CLASSIC

IQ TESTS

CLASSIC

IQ TESTS

By Philip J. Carter, Kenneth A. Russell,
and Fraser Simpson

Main Street
A division of Sterling Publishing Co., Inc.
New York

10 9 8 7 6 5 4 3 2 1

Published by Sterling Publishing Co., Inc.
387 Park Avenue South, New York, NY 10016
© 2005 by Sterling Publishing Co., Inc.

Material in this collection adapted from:
IQ Tests to Keep You Sharp, © 2002 by Philip J. Carter & Kenneth A. Russell
Brain-Flexing IQ Tests, © 2002 by Fraser Simpson

Distributed in Canada by Sterling Publishing
c/o Canadian Manda Group, 165 Dufferin Street
Toronto, Ontario, Canada M6K 3H6
Distributed in Great Britain by Chrysalis Books Group PLC
The Chrysalis Building, Bramley Road, London W10 6SP, England
Distributed in Australia by Capricorn Link (Australia) Pty. Ltd.
P.O. Box 704, Windsor, NSW 2756, Australia

Printed in China

Sterling ISBN 1-4027-1672-9

CLASSIC
IQ TESTS

CONTENTS

INTRODUCTION

The tests in this book are specially compiled to provide fun and entertainment to those who take them. At the same time, the questions are designed to be similar in format to those you are likely to encounter in IQ tests. If you perform well on these tests you are likely to do well on actual IQ tests. Because they have been specially compiled for this publication, the tests are not standardized and, therefore, an actual IQ score cannot be given. Nevertheless, we do provide an approximate guide to performance on each test, for those of you who may wish to exercise your competitive instincts. We also provide a time limit for those of you wishing to try the tests against the clock.

An IQ test usually consists of several different types of questions. These are basically verbal, numerical, visual (culture fair), and logic. To help you test yourself in each of these disciplines separately, and identify individual strengths and possible weaknesses which need to be worked on, we have arranged the tests in the book into five sections: verbal, visual, numerical, calculation and logic, and multidiscipline. The verbal, numerical, and calculation and logic sections consist of five individual tests with fifteen questions in each test. The visual section consists of three tests with fifteen questions each. The final section, IQ Testers, which brings together all the four types of questions in the previous sections, consists of twenty individual tests with fifteen questions in each test.

Scoring chart per test (each correct answer scores 1 point):

15	Genius level
14	Mastermind
13	Exceptional
11–12	Excellent
9–10	Very good
7–8	Good
5–6	Average

Warm Ups (verbal, visual, numerical*, calculation and logic)
Time limit: 40 minutes per test

IQ Testers
Time limit: 30 minutes per test

---

*Calculators may be used for these questions. It will not invalidate your score.

WARM UPS

VERBAL TEST 1

✦✦✦

1. Complete the six words so that the same two letters that end the first word start the second and the same two letters that end the second start the third word, etc. The same two letters that end the sixth word start the first word to complete the circle.

    _ _ **MI** _ _
    _ _ **AS** _ _
    _ _ **S I** _ _
    _ _ **F I** _ _
    _ _ **NG** _ _
    _ _ **RE** _ _

2. My energy is such that an oscillatory motion is taking place within my every roller-shaped chamber caused by the ignition of an explosive mixture. What am I doing?

3. CELEBRATE TEA-RIOT is an anagram of which two words that are ten-letters and six-letters long and opposite in meaning?

4. "An indirect, ingenious, and often cunning means to gain an end." What word fits closest to this definition?

SHENANIGAN, ARTIFICE, SUBTERFUGE, PLOT, SOPHISM

5. Work from letter to letter horizontally, vertically, or diagonally to spell out a seventeen-letter phrase.

L	I	A		
K	F	T		
E	H	E	O	N
		S	R	I
		E	K	L

6. Which two words are closest in meaning?

LOYAL, GRACIOUS, CONFIDENT, SALUBRIOUS, CORDIAL, COMELY

7. Place a word in the parentheses so that it makes a new word, phrase, or hyphenated word when added to the end of the first word, and makes another new word, phrase, or hyphenated word when placed in front of the second word.

CANNON (_ _ _ _) BEARINGS

8. Join three of the two-letter groups together to make a six-letter word that is a TREE.

IA, AC, CA, IN, AC, TK, PI, NA

9. Which word means the same as ERUBESCENT?

CHUBBY, BLUSHING, SPOTTY, CHARMING, JEALOUS, ENVIOUS

10. Which five-letter word can be placed at the end of these six words to make new words or phrases?

CLUB
DOLL
GREEN
FULL   (_ _ _ _ _)
SAFE
PENT

11. Find a six-letter word using only these five letters.

W   G

    I

L   E

12. What is the longest word that you can find by moving from square to square and only using each letter once? The answer is a ten-letter word.

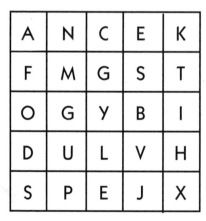

A	N	C	E	K
F	M	G	S	T
O	G	Y	B	I
D	U	L	V	H
S	P	E	J	X

13. Complete the three-letter words to make an eight-letter word on the bottom line.

S	E	A	A	C	E	A	A
O	R	S	S	U	G	D	R

14. Fill in the blanks to make two eight-letter words that are synonyms. You can go clockwise or counterclockwise.

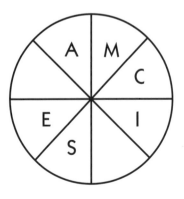
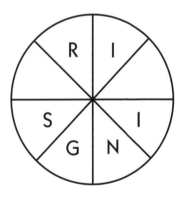

15. Find the starting point and track from letter to letter along
the lines to find the name of a country (5,3,6).

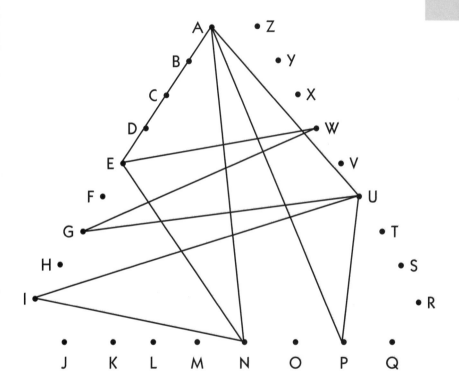

VERBAL TEST 2

1. Which word is the most opposite in meaning to PITHY?

**MERCIFUL, ABJECT, LOQUACIOUS,
COMICAL, SUCCINCT, EXPLICIT**

2. Which word will fit in front of these words to make new words?

	OWED
	EAR
(_ _ _)	**LESS**
	LONG
	ANGER

3. Read clockwise to figure out this sixteen-letter word. Only alternate letters are shown, and you have to find the starting point.

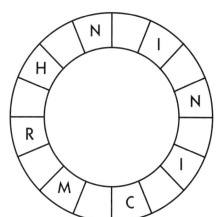

4. Which word is the odd one out?

DECODE, TRANSLATE, ENCIPHER, INTERPRET, REVEAL

5. Move a word from the right-hand column to the words in the left-hand column.

CAP	**BOOK**
MARE	**DREAM**
OWL	**GOWN**
SHADE	**BREAK**
?	

6. Add one letter, not necessarily the same letter, to each word in the front, end, or middle to find two words that are similar in meaning.

NICE   LACE

7. Change just one letter in each of the four words to spell out a familiar phrase.

SEAL   LINE   HIT   CARES

8. Find two words which mean the opposite.

MALADROIT, DEXTROUS, IGNOMINY,

NECESSARY, STUPEFY, MODERATION

9. Join two of the four-letter groups together to make an eight-letter word which is an ANIMAL.

MAND, CHIN, RILE, TIGE, CAPU, CHIL

10. What is the name given to a group of EAGLES?

(a) SIMPLICITY   (b) HILL   (c) CONVOCATION

(d) DRAUGHT   (e) PLUMP

11. Take one letter from each animal (in order) to make another animal.

POSSUM	DONKEY
ERMINE	KITTEN
RHESUS	CAYMAN

12. Which word will fit in front of these words to make new words or phrases?

CAKE

BOWL

(_ _ _ _)   HOOK

KNIFE

NET

TAIL

13. The vowels A, E, I, O, and U have been removed from this trite saying. See if you can replace them.

NYNWH   THNKS   THRSS   MGDNV   RYNHS

NTNTR   VWDNG   HPPL

14. Find a nine-letter word by starting at a corner and spiraling to the center.

15. Fill in the blanks to find an eight-letter word. You can go clockwise or counterclockwise.

VERBAL TEST 3

1. Which two words are the most opposite in meaning?

AMBIGUOUS, NECESSARY, DESTITUTE, INEVITABLE, SUPERFLUOUS, UNUSUAL

2. Place the letters in the correct boxes in each quadrant to obtain two eight-letter words, one reading clockwise and the other counterclockwise. The two words are antonyms.

NE: ENNP
SE: ORAN
SW: IPPT
NW: STOA

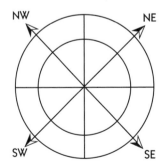

3. **PRONGHORN : ANTELOPE**
   HELLBENDER :

   (a) SNAKE   (b) COUGAR   (c) SALAMANDER
   (d) SPIDER   (e) STICKLEBACK

4. With the aid of the clue below, find two words that form a palindrome, i.e., a phrase that reads the same backwards and forwards. For example: HIGHEST BILLING = TOP SPOT.

   WICKED FRUIT

5. What is the longest word in the English language that can be produced from the following ten letters?

   ACEIMNORVW

6. Place two letters in each pair of words so that they finish the word on the left and start the word on the right. The letters in the parentheses reading in pairs downwards will spell out an eight-letter word.

   RI (_ _) AR
   CO (_ _) ER
   LA (_ _) AR
   OV (_ _) LY

7. Make a six-letter word using only these four letters.

E   R

U   D

8. Which word means the opposite of NEGATION?

**(a) DEBATABLE   (b) MOROSE   (c) INFLUENCE
(d) AFFIRMATION   (e) MUSTINESS**

9. Join two of the three-letter groups together to make a six-letter word which is an HERB.

RET, VES, GAR, SOR, CHI, LIK

10. Complete the word.

_ _ UBRE _ _ _

Clue: Found on the stage

11. Rearrange these words to make a trite saying.

MIDDLE	THAN	FAT	MENACED
FAT	THE	BY	IT
AROUND	THE	SOCIETY	IS
IS	THE	LESS	EARS
THREATENED	THE	BY	BETWEEN

12. Fill in the blanks to find two words which are antonyms. You can go clockwise or counterclockwise.

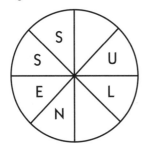 

13. Add one letter, not necessarily the same letter, to these words to find six new words all on the same theme.

CAP, CAB, ACE, CHB, NET

14. What is the longest word that you can find by moving from square to square and only using each letter once? The answer is a ten-letter word.

B	J	N	Q	U
A	T	E	W	F
M	D	H	P	X
R	I	G	Y	O
V	L	K	S	C

15. Find two sports by placing the letters in the squares.

E	C	F
E	G	I
I	K	N
N	R	T

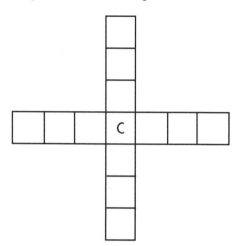

VERBAL TEST 4

1. Only one set of letters below can be arranged into a five-letter English word. Can you find the word?

N U T R P

E B N P L

O G P N E

H I R C T

S A B T L

U N T G E

M U R D O

E N T U C

M N T E L

E P L O N

2. Which word comes closest in meaning to PROSAIC?

DELIBERATE, BANAL, ANCIENT, UNUSUAL, DISCORDANT

3. Only ten letters of the alphabet do not appear in the array below. What ten-letter phrase can be spelled out from the missing letters?

W	**M**	**Y**	**J**
G	**Z**	**O**	**Q**
K	**T**	**F**	**N**
P	**X**	**L**	**H**

Clue: Might this person occasionally get that sinking feeling?

4. A quotation by Louis Pasteur has been split into three-letter groups which have then been arranged into random order. Can you put the letters in the correct order and reveal the quotation?

PRE, ORS, IND, CHA, THE, EDM, FAV, PAR, NCE

5. Working clockwise, take one letter from each circle in turn to spell out two synonyms.

Clue: Each word starts in a different circle.

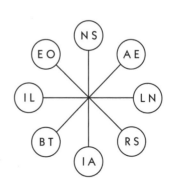

6. RATTLE PUFFY MICE is an anagram of which two words that are similar in meaning (6, 9)?

7. Start at one of the corner squares and spiral clockwise to the center letter to spell out a nine-letter word. You have to provide the missing letters.

8. The vowels A, E, I, O, and U have been omitted from this trite saying. See if you can replace them.

**THWRL   DGTSB   TTRVR   YDYTH   NWRSG
NNTHV   NNG**

9. Which two words are the closest in meaning?

PERMEATED, OBSTINATE, CORPOREAL, TRIFLING, PRODIGIOUS, DOGGED

10. What is a CARAPACE?

(a) A SHELL   (b) A BODKIN   (c) A MIDGET
(d) A HAYSTACK   (e) A MEASURE

11. Join three sets of the three letters to make two nine-letter words.

SEC, ECT, RET, IVE, INV, ION

12. Which word means the opposite of SABLE?

(a) AWKWARD
(b) BURDEN
(c) ACUTE
(d) BLACK
(e) WHITE

13. Fill in the blanks to find two eight-letter words which are synonyms. You can go clockwise or counterclockwise.

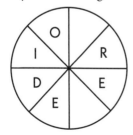 

14. Complete the three-letter words to make an eight-letter word in the bottom line.

A	E	A	H	S	A	E	W
S	M	S	I	K	R	R	I

15. Find an eight-letter word by filling in the blanks. You can go clockwise or counterclockwise.

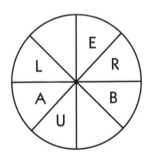

VERBAL TEST 5

1. Six synonyms of the word PARTNER are shown. Take one letter from each of the synonyms (in order) to find another synonym of PARTNER.

ASSOCIATE, SPOUSE, COMPANION, HUSBAND, COLLEAGUE, COMRADE, MATE

2. If meat in a river is T(HAM)ES, can you find a brave man in a Native American tribe?

3. Insert a word in the parentheses that means the same as the definitions outside the parentheses.

Barred frame (   ) Grind noisily

4. Find four six-letter words with the aid of the clues. The same three letters in each word are represented by XYZ, which is a familiar three-letter word.

X Y Z _ _ _	**Overthrow**
_ X Y Z _ _	**A place of ideal perfection**
_ _ X Y Z _	**Prevents**
_ _ _ X Y Z	**Type of computer**

5. Insert an American city into the bottom line to complete the nine three-letter words.

F	T	A	A	P	W	P	R	B
I	O	R	S	I	A	A	U	A

6. Use each letter of this newspaper headline only once to spell out three kinds of precious minerals.

LAZY ATTEMPTS - OH DEAR ME!

7. Take one letter from each circle in turn to spell out five foods.

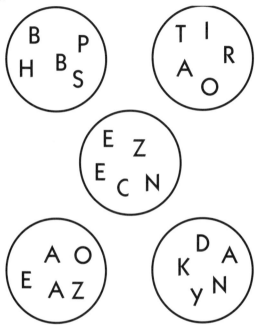

8. Place a word in the parentheses which means the same as the two words outside the parentheses.

ASSISTANT (_ _ _ _ _ _) RUNNER-UP

9. Find a one-word anagram for DREAM LILT.

10. Put four out of these five two-letter groups together to make an eight-letter fish.

OU   ER   AI   ND   FL

11. Find a nine-letter word using only these four letters.

N A
S I

12. Fill in the blanks to find two eight-letter words which are synonyms. You can go clockwise or counterclockwise.

 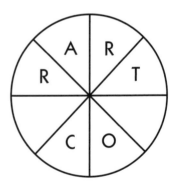

13. Spell out a ten-letter word by moving into each circle only once.

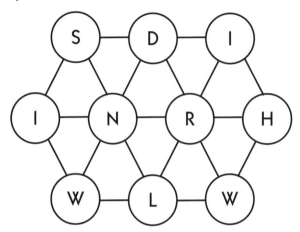

Clue: Inclement weather

14. Rearrange these boxes to make a trite saying.

WORMS	TO	A	ONLY
ONCE	TO	USE	THE
OF	RECAN	CAN	A
YOU	CAN	CAN	THEM
OPEN	IS	WAY	LONGER

15. Fill in the blanks to find a ten-letter word. You can go clockwise or counterclockwise.

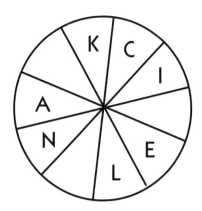

VISUAL TEST 1

1. What comes next in the sequence?

   ?

A.   **B.**   **C.**   **D.**   **E.**

2.   is to

as

 is to

A.   **B.**   **C.**   **D.**   **E.**   **F.**

3. Which is the odd one out?

A.   **B.**   **C.**

D.   **E.**   **F.**

4. **EE** is to **F6**

as

Ct is to

CE	**Гb**	**EE**	**C6**	**Г8**
A.	**B.**	**C.**	**D.**	**E.**

5. Which is the odd one out?

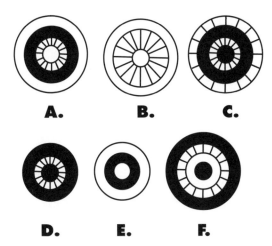

A.   B.   C.

D.   E.   F.

6.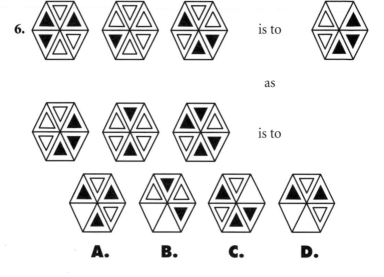

is to

as

is to

A.   **B.**   **C.**   **D.**

7. Which symbol is missing from the circle?

A.   **B.**   **C.**   **D.**   **E.**

8. What comes next in the sequence?

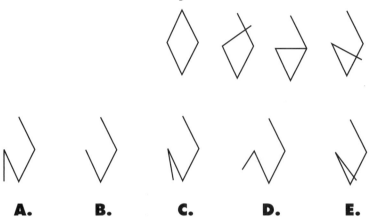

A. **B.** **C.** **D.** **E.**

9. Which is the odd one out?

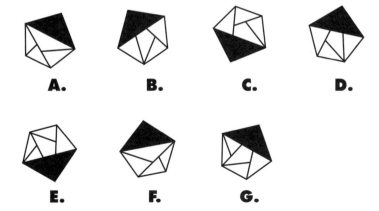

A. **B.** **C.** **D.**

E. **F.** **G.**

10.   is to

as

    is to

            (D.)

A.   **B.**   **C.**   **D.**

11. Which design should replace the question mark?

            ?

A.   **B.**   **C.**

12. Which is the odd one out?

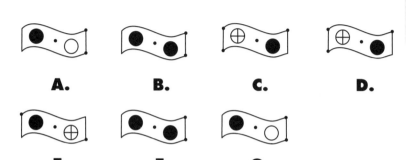

A.   **B.**   **C.**   **D.**

E.   **F.**   **G.**

13.

What comes next in the above sequence?

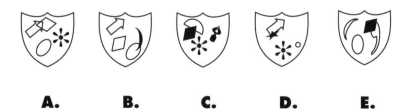

A.   **B.**   **C.**   **D.**   **E.**

14. What is the total of the numbers on the reverse side of these dice?

15. What is the average area of the 7 shapes in square units?

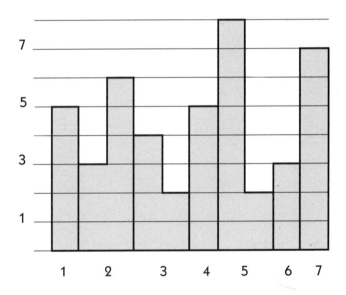

VISUAL TEST 2

1. 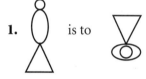 is to

as

is to

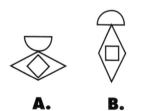

A. **B.** **C.** **D.** **E.**

47

2.

      ?

What comes next in the above sequence?

A.   **B.**   **C.**   **D.**   **E.**

3. Which is the odd one out?

A.   **B.**   **C.**   **D.**   **E.**

4. What comes next in the sequence?

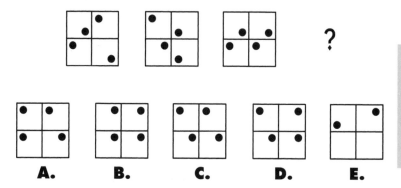

5. Which square should replace the question mark?

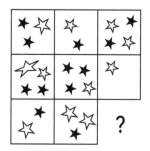

6.

What comes next in the sequence?

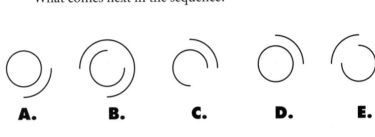

A. **B.** **C.** **D.** **E.**

7. The contents of which shield below are most like the contents of the shield to the right?

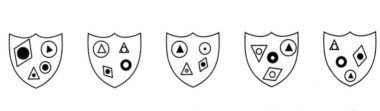

A. **B.** **C.** **D.** **E.**

8. Which is the odd one out?

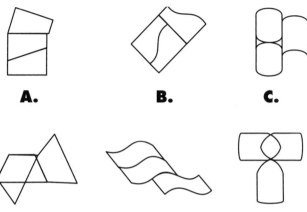

A.   **B.**   **C.**

D.   **E.**   **F.**

9.

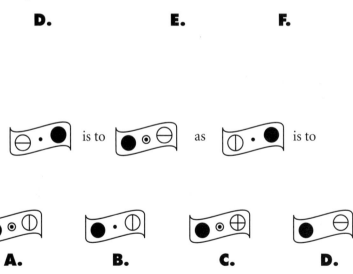

A.   **B.**   **C.**   **D.**

10. If   &*+#   is to   +#&*

Then   +>#=   is to   ?

A. =>+#   **B.** #=+>

C. #+>=   **D.** =>+#

11. Which is the odd one out?

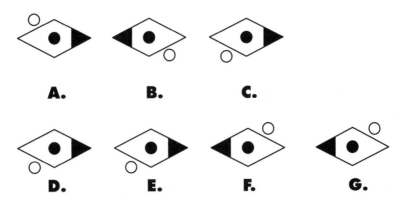

12. Which circle should replace the question mark?

R S T

X

Y

Z

A. **B.** **C.** **D.** **E.**

13. Each line and symbol that appears in the four outer circles is transferred to the center circle according to these rules:

If a line or symbol occurs in the outer circles:
  once, then it is transferred.
  twice, then it is possibly transferred.
  three times, then it is transferred.
  four times, then it is not transferred.

Which of the circles A, B, C, D, or E shown below should appear at the center of the diagram above?

A. **B.** **C.** **D.** **E.**

14. Which is the odd one out?

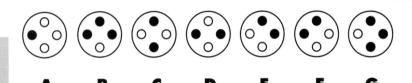

A.   B.   C.   D.   E.   F.   G.

15. What is the total value of these three angles?

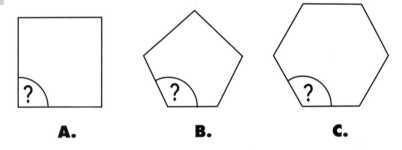

A.   B.   C.

VISUAL TEST 3

✦✦✦

1. Which is the odd one out?

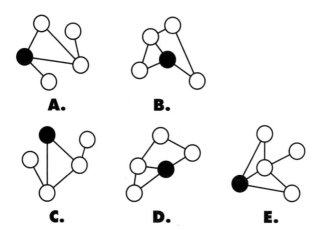

A.

B.

C.

D.

E.

2. is to

as

 is to

A.

B.

C.

D.

E.

3. How many lines appear at the right?

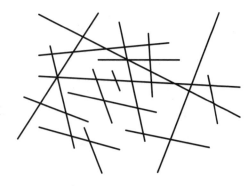

4. Which is the odd one out?

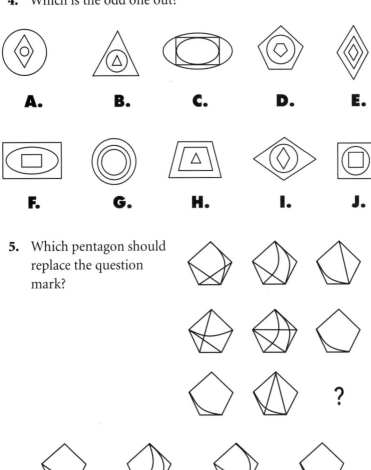

A.   **B.**   **C.**   **D.**   **E.**

F.   **G.**   **H.**   **I.**   **J.**

5. Which pentagon should replace the question mark?

?

A.   **B.**   **C.**   **D.**

6. Which is the odd one out?

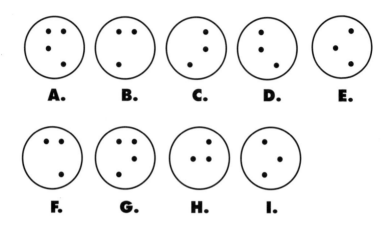

A.   **B.**   **C.**   **D.**   **E.**

F.   **G.**   **H.**   **I.**

7. To which of the squares below can a dot be added so that the dot then meets the same conditions as the dot in the square to the right?

A.   **B.**   **C.**   **D.**   **E.**

8. Which hexagon should replace the question mark?

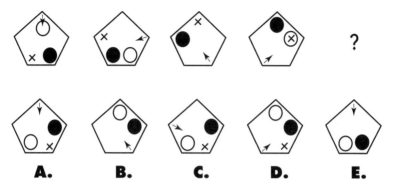

?

9. Which is the odd one out?

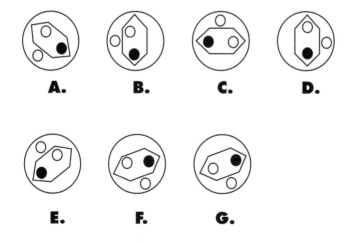

10.

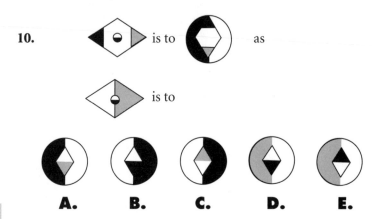

11. Each line and symbol that appears in the four outer circles is transferred to the center circle according to these rules:

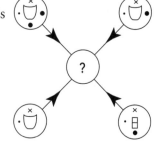

> If a line or symbol occurs in the outer circles:
>   once, then it is transferred.
>   twice, then it is possibly transferred.
>   three times, then it is transferred.
>   four times, then it is not transferred.

Which of the circles A, B, C, D, or E shown below should appear at the center of the diagram above?

12. Each pair of circles produces the circle above by carrying forward only those elements that are different. Similar elements are canceled out. Which circle should replace the question mark?

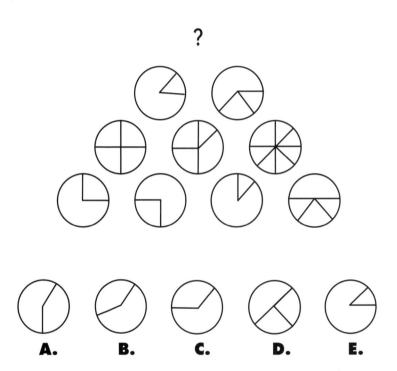

A.   **B.**   **C.**   **D.**   **E.**

13. Each of the nine squares in the grid marked 1A to 3C should incorporate all the lines and symbols which are shown in the squares of the same letter and number above and to the left. For example, 2B should incorporate all the lines and symbols that are in 2 and B.

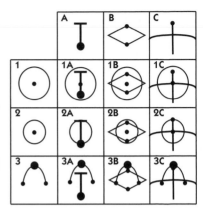

One of the squares is incorrect. Which one is it?

14. Which symbol should replace the question mark?

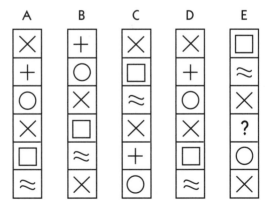

15. Which circle should replace the question mark?

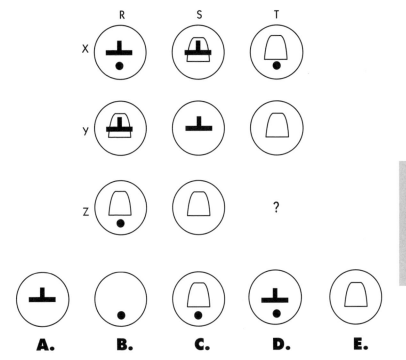

NUMERICAL TEST 1

◆◆◆

1. What number should replace the question mark?

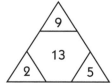 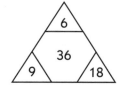 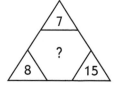

2. What number comes next in the sequence below?

3624, 4363, 3644, 4563, 3664, ?

3. What number should replace the question mark?

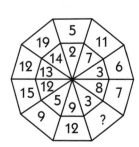

4. What four digits should appear in the middle section?

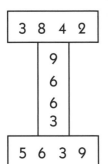

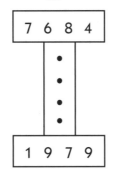

5 2 1 7
9
4
8
1
4 3 8 1

5. What number should replace the question mark?

	2				**4**				**?**	
7	**4**	**4**		**6**	**9**	**5**		**3**	**8**	**6**

6. Each line of numbers follows the same logical progression. Replace the question marks with the correct numbers.

3 8 2 4	1 1 6	?

4 9 6 8	?	1 8

7 5 1 9	?	?

7. Which number is the odd one out?

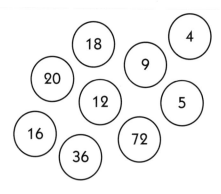

8. A man caught a fish. It weighed ⁵⁄₇ kg + ⁵⁄₇ its own weight. What did it weigh?

9. What number should replace the question mark?

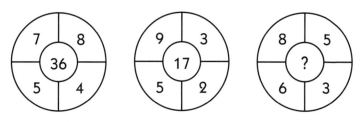

10. What fraction will produce this recurring decimal?

.166166166....

11. Which number should replace the question mark?

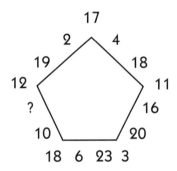

12. What number should replace the question mark?

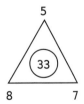 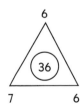 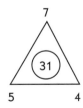 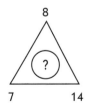

13. What number should replace the question mark?

4	2	9	8	6
3	8	7	9	5
8	1	7	?	1

14. What number comes next?

0, 1, 3, 6, 7, 9, 12, 13, ?

15. What number should replace the question mark?

8	9	3	69
7	5	6	29
4	7	9	19
9	8	4	?

NUMERICAL TEST 2

1. Multiply by 7 the number of odd numbers that are immediately followed by an even number in the row of numbers below. What is the answer?

4 2 8 7 5 3 2 5 1 7 4 6 8 1 4 2 5 7 6 8 3 1 9

2. What number is two places away from itself less 3, two places away from itself plus 2, two places away from itself plus 4, three places away from itself less 1, and three places away from itself less 5?

10	24	1	27	9
2	11	5	7	3
29	16	25	12	18
17	14	8	4	13
9	20	22	6	15

NUMERICAL
Test 2

3. What number should replace the question mark?

4. What number should replace the question mark?

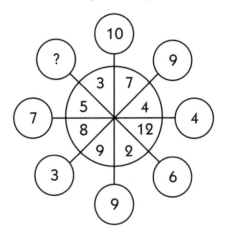

5. What number should replace the question mark?

2836 : 13
9423 : 14
7229 : ?

6. What number should replace the question mark?

7	4	5	3
1	6	3	7
3	8	1	7
6	1	8	?

7. What number should replace the question mark?

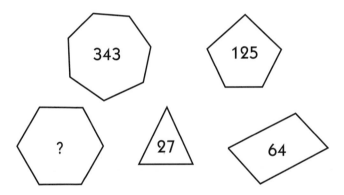

8. The average of three numbers is 24.
The average of two numbers of these three numbers is 22½.
What is the value of the third number?

9. If a test score goes up 15% from x to 69, what was the previous test score?

10. What number should replace the question mark?

27, 27, 30¼, 23¾, 33½, 20½, 36¾, 17¼, ?

11. What number should replace the question mark?

39	3	4	9
54	6	8	6
45	36	9	1
35	7	7	?

12. What number should replace the question mark?

13. What number should replace the question mark?

1st	2nd	3rd	4th
26	27	29	25
28	29	31	36
30	31	37	49
32	33	?	64
34	35	43	81

NUMERICAL
Test 2

14. Which is the odd one out?

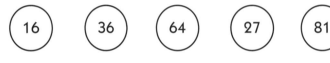

A. 16   **B.** 36   **C.** 64   **D.** 27   **E.** 81

15. What number should replace the question mark?

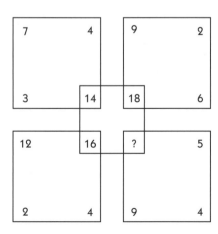

NUMERICAL TEST 3

♦ ♦ ♦

1. **6, 50, 402, 3218, ?**

   What number comes next in the above sequence?

2. What number should replace the question mark?

3. What number should replace the question mark?

4. What number should replace the question mark?

```
        8           6
    3       8           7
5       4       8           5
2       9       4           7
    ?       5           4
        5       9
```

5. What number should replace the question mark?

4322 : 48
4172 : 56
7615 : ?

6. What number should replace the question mark?

  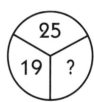

7. Which two numbers, one in the top rectangle and one in the bottom rectangle, are the odd ones out?

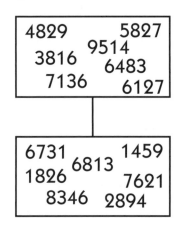

8. Find the value of x:

$$(16)(3^2) = (2^3)x$$

9. Simplify

$$(87^2) - (86^2)$$

10. What number should replace the question mark?

17	26	21	30
38	29	34	25
33	42	37	?

11.

If

is   LM   NO   LP   NQ

What is   ?

12. What number should replace the question mark?

| 7 | 12 | 9 |

| 13 | 18 | 15 |

| 11 | 16 | 13 |

| 17 | 22 | ? |

13. What number should replace the question mark?

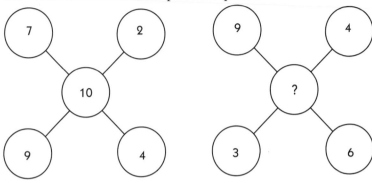

14. What number should replace the question mark?

42	7	6	12
91	13	4	11
88	11	5	13
27	9	8	?

15. What number should replace the question mark?

16	23	28	38	?

NUMERICAL TEST 4

♦♦♦

1. What number should replace the question mark?

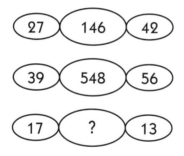

2. What number should replace the question mark?

```
?
5   3
3   3   1
2   1   2   1
1   1   1   1   1
```

3. What number should replace the question mark?

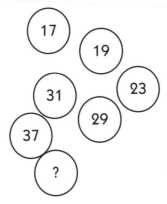

4. What number should replace the question mark?

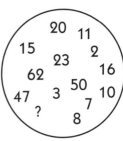

5. These numbers are in logical groupings. What number should replace the question mark?

	7			5			6	
8		3	7		5	?		6
2		9	1		5	1		6

6. What numbers should appear on the bottom row?

2	4	3	7	11
10	5	13	9	7
22	23	17	19	18
?	?	?	?	?

7. Simplify and find the value for x:

$$X = \frac{1}{\dfrac{2}{3} - \dfrac{1}{2}}$$

8. What fraction will produce this recurring decimal?

.71288888888888 . . .

9. What should replace the question mark?

82, 82, 86¼, 77¾, 90½, 73½, 94¾, 69¼, ?

10. Simplify to find the value of x:

$$x = (-5) - (-7) - (-2)$$

11. What is the value of the angle in an octagon?

12. What number should replace the question mark?

6	7	4	52
8	5	3	39
4	3	8	56
5	2	4	?

13. What number should replace the question mark?

14. What value weight should be placed at the question mark to balance the scale?

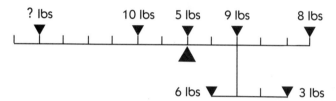

15.

KL   MN   KP   MQ   KQ

What is the code for this symbol ?

NUMERICAL TEST 5

1. What number comes next?

   7, 12, 20, 34, 60, ?

2. What number should replace the question mark?

7	4	3	25
6	2	4	8
7	8	5	51
3	9	8	?

3. Which of these numbers is the odd one out?

   2446   **2137**

   8429   **3248**   **6379**

   2483   **1226**

   5687

4. Multiply the third-highest odd number in the left-hand group with the third-lowest even number in the right-hand group. What is the answer?

37	42	96	44	23	46	59	56	89	18
64	35	21	39	59	69	52	50	11	72
56	31	78	58	16	37	15	68	92	25
26	47	34	74	29	51	44	19	82	54
66	33	84	27	68	48	11	27	26	21

5. What number should replace the question mark?

45 (2) 52

97 (7) 33

67 (?) 72

6. What number comes next?

1, 1, 3, 6, 5, 11, 7, ?

7. What number should replace the question mark?

4812 : 72

7324 : 13

9417 : ?

8. What number should replace the question mark?

9. What number should replace the question mark?

10. What number should replace the question mark?

11. What number should replace the question mark?

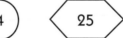

12. What number should replace the question mark?

13. What number should replace the question mark?

14. Simplify

$$^{17}/_{19} \div {}^{68}/_{38} \div {}^{16}/_{32}$$

15. Place the correct numbers in the vacant pyramid bricks.

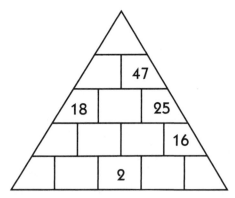

Each brick is the total of the two bricks that are supporting it. (One number is −6.)

CALCULATION AND LOGIC
TEST 1

1. What letter is two to the right of the letter immediately to the left of the letter three to the right of the letter C?

A B C D E F G H

2. How many minutes is it before 12 noon if 55 minutes ago it was four times as many minutes past 8 AM as it is minutes before noon now?

3. Sid is one-and-a-half times as old as Alf who is one-and-a-half times as old as Jim. Their combined ages total 133. How old are the three men?

4. The following words are in a logical progression:

PAINT

UMPIRE

FANATIC

DARKNESS

Which word comes next?

**ABDICATED, TRUCULENT, GARDENING,
THROUGHOUT, CHIEFTAIN, ARILLODE**

5. If five lemons and two oranges cost $4.60 and two lemons
and three oranges cost $3.60, what is the cost of an orange
and what is the cost of a lemon?

6. My watch showed the correct time at 12 noon, but then the
battery started to run down until it eventually stopped completely. Between 12 noon up to its stopping, it lost 15 minutes per hour on average. It now shows 6 PM, but it stopped
3 hours ago. What is the correct time now?

7. You have picked 667 apples from the trees in your orchard,
which you are putting into bags to give your neighbors. You
wish to put an equal number of apples into each bag, and
you wish to use as few bags as possible. How many apples
should you put into how many bags?

8. A number plus ⅖ of that number, plus 6, minus 4¹⁄₂₅ is 3²⁄₂₅. What is the number?

9. How do you change Celsius to Fahrenheit and vice versa?

10. An assistant was slicing bacon. He sliced each slab of bacon into 16 slices at the rate of 60 slices per minute. How many slabs had he chopped up after 20 minutes?

11. Two square floors had to be covered in 12-in. tiles. The number of tiles used was 850. Each side of one floor was 10 ft. more than the other floor. What were the dimensions of the two floors?

12. In 9 years' time the combined age of my four brothers will be 99. What will it be in 11 years' time?

13. Which is the odd one out?

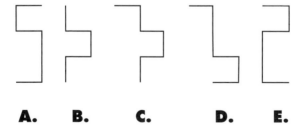

A.   B.   C.   D.   E.

14. At the boarding school, three sisters travel home regularly. One travels every 5 days, one travels every 6 days, and one travels every 7 days. When will they all return to the school at the same time?

15. Five friends live in street-corner buildings in New York City. Where should they meet in order to cut down their walking time to a minimum?

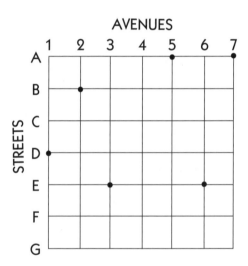

CALCULATION AND LOGIC
TEST 2

1. Al beats Bill at chess but loses to Hillary. Chelsea usually wins against Bill but never against Hillary. Who is the weakest player?

2. What comes next in the sequence?

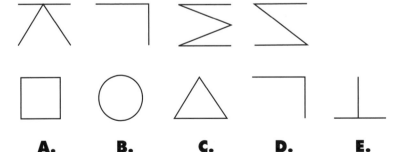

93

3. **FINAL (FLIRT) ENTER**

Using the same logic as in the example above, what word is coded to appear in the bracket below?

BIKER (_ _ _ _ _) RIFLE

4. A train traveling at a speed of 75 mph enters a tunnel 1.25 miles long. The length of the train is 0.25 miles. How long does it take for all of the train to pass through the tunnel, from the moment the front enters to the moment the rear emerges?

5. If a man weighs 75% of his own weight plus 42 lbs., how much does he weigh?

6. Frasier had twice as many as Niles, and Niles had twice as many as Daphne. But then Daphne lost one of hers, and of the ones she then had left, she gave twice as many to Frasier as she gave to Niles. This meant that Frasier still had less than 20, but still had twice as many as Niles.

How many did each have originally?

7. These clocks follow a weird kind of logic. What time should the fourth clock face show?

8. The dog and kennel cost more than $20. If the dog had cost $5 more, the kennel would have cost $\frac{1}{3}$ of the total. If the kennel had cost $5 less, I would have spent $\frac{3}{4}$ of the total on the dog.

    What was the cost of the dog?

9. A large square had an area of 490 sq. ft. It was the same area as two smaller squares. One had a side that was 3 times the length of the other.

    What were the areas of the two smaller squares?

10. Ten people shared a birthday cake. They all had equal portions and yet one piece remained on the plate.

    How was this possible?

11. Replace the letters with numbers so that the sum is correct.

S L O W
S L O W
+ O L D
―――――
OW L S

12. I had a 99-year lease; ⅔ of the time past was equal to ⅘ of the time to come.

How much of the lease had expired?

13. The combined ages of:

Alice and Barbara is 76.

Alice and Chloe is 96.

Barbara and Chloe is 140.

How old are Alice, Barbara, and Chloe?

14. Find the weight to balance the scale.

15. Four cheeses of different sizes are placed on Stool A. How many moves will it take to move the cheeses one by one to Stool C? A cheese must not be placed on a cheese smaller than itself.

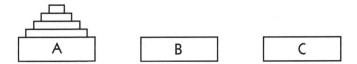

CALCULATION AND LOGIC
TEST 3

1. Jack and Jill share their sweets in the ratio of 3:8. If Jill has 56 sweets, how many does Jack have?

2. You are trying to fill your bathtub with both hot and cold water, but you accidentally forgot to put the stopper in the drain. The hot tap takes 4.5 minutes to fill the bath. The cold tap takes 12 minutes to fill the bath. The plug hole takes 18 minutes to empty a full bath.

   How long will it take for the bath to fill completely?

3. In my wardrobe all but four of my jackets are brown, all but four are blue, all but four are gray, all but four are green, and all but four are black. How many jackets do I have altogether?

4. Your boss offers you a choice of two options by which your new salary is to be calculated.

First option: Initial salary $40,000 to be increased after each 12 months by $2000.

Second option: Initial salary $40,000 to be increased after each 6 months by $500.

The salary will be calculated every six months.

Which option should you choose?

5. Four playing cards are placed in a row. The King of Hearts is next to the Ace of Spades, but not next to the Three of Diamonds. The Three of Diamonds is not next to the Nine of Clubs. Which card is next to the Nine of Clubs?

6. Between fifty and a hundred people hired a private carriage for a railway trip. They paid a total of $2847. Each person paid the same amount, which was an exact number of dollars. How many people went on the trip?

7. There are a number of lions and eagles at the zoo. In all, they have 30 heads and 86 legs. How many lions and how many eagles are there?

8. Which day is two days after the day four days before the day immediately following the day two days before Saturday?

SUNDAY

MONDAY

TUESDAY

WEDNESDAY

THURSDAY

FRIDAY

SATURDAY

9. My friend lives on a long road where the numbers of the houses run consecutively from 1 to 82. To find his number, I asked him three questions to which I received either a "yes" or "no" answer to each. The questions were:

1. Is it under 41?

2. Is it divisible by 4?

3. Is it a square number?

My friend answered "yes" twice and "no" once. From my friend's answers, I was able to determine for certain what the house number was. What is the house number?

10. At a golf club, Man A challenged Man B to a match. Man A scored 72, Man B scored 69. Man A won, but it was not match play. How was that possible?

11. I am thinking of a number between 99 and 999.

1. The number is below 500.

2. It is a square number.

3. It is a cube number.

4. The first and last digits are 5, 7, or 9.

One of the first three statements is a lie. What is the number?

12. I asked my son to tell me how many stamps he had. He replied, "The number if divided by 2 will give a remainder of 1, divided by 3 a remainder of 2, by 4 a remainder of 3, by 5 a remainder of 4, by 6 a remainder of 5, by 7 a remainder of 6, by 8 a remainder of 7, by 9 a remainder of 8, by 10 a remainder of 9."

How many stamps did he have, if he had fewer than 5,000 stamps?

13. Arthur and Bert built the brickwork of a house in 24 days. If Arthur can do only two-thirds as much as Bert, how long would it take each of them working alone?

14. Replace the letters with numbers so that the product is correct.

$$
\begin{array}{r}
\mathsf{W\ HAT} \\
\times\quad\ \mathsf{A} \\
\hline
\mathsf{SHOW}
\end{array}
$$

15. A man left a sum of money to his three children. Albert is to get 20% more than Jasper and 25% more than Cyril. Jasper's share is $3600. How much does Cyril get?

CALCULATION AND LOGIC
TEST 4

◆◆◆

1. Insert the numbers 1 to 6 into the circles so that for any particular circle the sum of numbers in the circles connected directly to it equals the value corresponding to the number, as given in the list.

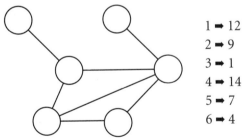

1 ➡ 12
2 ➡ 9
3 ➡ 1
4 ➡ 14
5 ➡ 7
6 ➡ 4

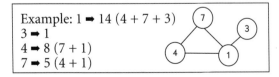

Example: 1 ➡ 14 (4 + 7 + 3)
3 ➡ 1
4 ➡ 8 (7 + 1)
7 ➡ 5 (4 + 1)

2. A man has 47 colored socks in his drawer: 14 identical blue socks, 23 identical red socks, and 10 identical gray. The lights have failed and he is left completely in the dark. How many socks must he take out of the drawer to be 100% certain he has at least one pair of each color?

3. In a game with 24 players that lasts for exactly 50 minutes, there are 24 players plus 8 reserves who alternate equally with each player. This means that all players, including reserves, are on the field for the same length of time. How long is that?

4. What number comes next?

3842971, 172483, 34271, ?

5. Divide 500 by a quarter and add 50. How many have you got?

6. In the morning, a news vendor sold two copies of one magazine and five copies of a newspaper for a total of $15. In the afternoon, he sold five copies of the same magazine and two copies of the same newspaper for a total of $18.60. What is the cost of one newspaper and one magazine?

7. The following words are in a logical progression:

PLACEBOS, SECLUDED, SPECIFIC

Which one of the following comes next?

**MAGAZINE, TOGETHER, CHIPMUNK,
ANYWHERE, BARITONE**

8. At the zoo the numbers of the animals' cages were:

LION   16
SEA LION   27
MONKEY   26
ANTELOPE   32

What is the number of the buffalo's cage?

9. A piece of land was up for sale at $50 per square yard. What will the cost be?

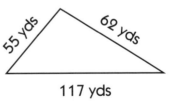

117 yds

10. At a holiday camp there were 38 holiday makers. There will be at least 19 people who are mutual friends, or at least 19 people who are mutual strangers. True or false?

11. WHAT IS THIS?

> Take half of this,
> and add one more.
> Then triple that,
> and add on four.
> But just the same
> result you'd see
> if now you had added 23.

12. A man started a business with $2,000 and increased his wealth by 50% every 3 years. How much did he possess after 18 years?

13. Deduct four thousand eleven hundred and a half from twelve thousand twelve hundred and twelve. What is the answer?

14. If you add the square of Tony's age to the age of Margaret, the sum is 62. If you add the square of Margaret's age to the age of Tony, the result is 176. What are Tony's and Margaret's ages?

15. Four burglars were being questioned by the police about a robbery.

> "Jack did it," said Alan.
> "George did it," said Jack.
> "It wasn't me," said Sid.
> "Jack is a liar if he said that I did it," said George.

Only one had spoken the truth. Who was the culprit?

CALCULATION AND LOGIC
TEST 5

✦✦✦

1. What letter is two to the left of the letter immediately to the right of the letter which is midway between the letter immediately to the right of the letter B and the letter immediately to the left of the letter H?

A   B   C   D   E   F   G   H

2. Tom, Dick, and Harry wish to share a certain sum of money among them. Tom gets ⅗, Dick gets 0.35, and Harry gets $325. How much is the original sum of money?

3. Harry is a one-and-a-quarter times Dick's age, and Dick is one-and-a-quarter times Tom's age. Their combined ages total 122. How old are the three men?

4. **3 8 7 2 5**   is to   **7 5 8 3 2**   as

   9 1 4 8 2   is to

   A. 18429 **B.** 13493 **C.** 24198 **D.** 49821 **E.** 42198

5. In a quiz show, the winner is allowed to pick four box numbers at random out of a total of ten boxes. Just four of the boxes contain a valuable prize, while six of the boxes contain something that is worthless. What are the chances that the contestant will be lucky enough to win all four of the valuable prizes?

6. Tom, Dick, and Harry have 84 among them. If Tom and Harry put theirs together, they have twice as many as Dick. If Dick and Harry put theirs together, they will have the same number as Tom. How many does each of them have?

7. Dallas, Texas, is 756 miles away from Detroit, Michigan. A nonstop train leaves Dallas traveling at 80 mph. Another nonstop train leaves Detroit at exactly the same time traveling at 90 mph. Which train will be farther from Dallas when they meet?

8. If   **61 → 55**
       23 → 21
       84 → 76

   What does 41 → ?

9. How many revolutions must the largest cog make in order to bring the cogs back to their original positions?

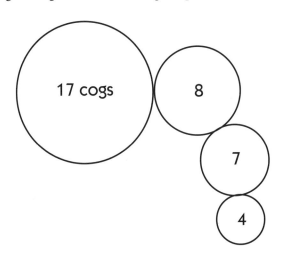

10. How many squares are there on an 8 × 8 square chessboard?

11. "Did you catch anything?" said Jill.

Her husband said, "A large fish. It weighed ⁶⁄₇ of its weight + ⅔ of a pound."

What did the fish weigh?

12. Find the missing number.

7	6	5	16
9	14	11	25
13	26	17	?
25	32	23	49

13. A said to B, "Here is my wallet. Give me the same amount of money as there is in the wallet." B counted the money and added to it the same amount. B said to A, "Give me as much as I have left and we will be all square." A said that he had $3.50 left. B said he had $3. How much did each possess at first?

14. Which number added to 100 and 164 will make them both perfect square numbers?

15. I knew an oldish lady in Dundee,
Whose age has its last digit "3."
The square of the first
Is her whole age reversed.
So what must the lady's age be?

IQ TESTERS

TEST 1

◆◆◆

1. Change one of the letters in one of the words in this sentence to make a word that fits in the blank.

Because of the flood, we ended up with water all over the basement _____.

2. Fill in the next domino in this sequence.

E	77	K	61	Q	45	
85	H	69	N	53	T	

3. On Sunday, Jack had 63 toys. Every day, starting on Sunday, he gave away half of his toys plus half a toy. On what day of the week did Jack give away his last toy?

4. Change one letter in each of these four words and then respace the result without rearranging the letters to make a piece of tactical advice.

DIVA   DEAL   ICON   SUER

5. One minute ago, a clock that strikes only the hours just finished striking an hour. If the clock has struck a total of 21 in the last 2½ hours, what hour did it just finish striking?

6. Which of A or B is equivalent to the original block rotated in three dimensions?

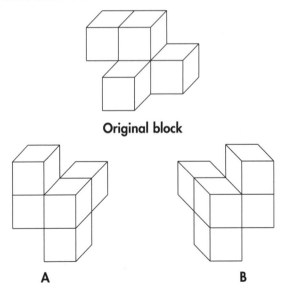

Original block

A   **B**

7. Add the same letter seven times (and appropriate spacing) to this string of letters and then respace the result to form four related words. You don't need to rearrange the letters in the string.

L A V I L E S A P U L A S A R U M O Y X

8. Rhyme time! If a shameless dried grape is a BRAZEN RAISIN, what would you call a little stone in the resistance movement?

9. Remove exactly half of the letters in the sentence below to reveal a two-word phrase described by the sentence itself. You don't have to rearrange any letters ... the answer is in the correct order from left to right.

BE A BIG WINNER—NO SLOUCH—A FLUKE

10. The numbers in the diagrams combine in the same way to make correct arithmetic statements. What number is missing from the last diagram?

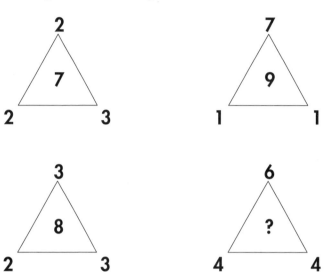

11. What comes next in this sequence?

O3   T3   T5   F4   F4   S3   S5   E5   ___

12. The number 865,469 is divisible by only one two-digit palindrome. Which one?

13. Three related words have been written in a row without spaces and with the vowels removed. What are the three words?

L   P   H   N   T   R   M   D   L   L   N   T   L   P

14. Rearrange the letters of each of these three words to form three related words.

CARTELS   _____

CRIMEAN   _____

MICRONS   _____

15. Insert the same four letters in each set of blanks to form flowers.

__ __ __ **I E** __

__ __ __ **A C** __

TEST 2

1. WORST SHEET can be rearranged to make the two words SHORT & SWEET. Rearrange these letters to make a different pair of "this & that" words.

NO INK, BESS

2. What single letter can be inserted into each of these words to form three new words?

RAGE SACK AREA

3. Every morning, Gillian goes to the store and buys 6 dog treats, and every evening she gives 3 treats to her dog. If Gillian has 30 dog treats in her house on June 1 before going to the store, on which date in June will she first have 60 dog treats in the house?

4. Match two of the lettered items with each picture in the bottom row by writing two letters in the blank. For example, if pictures **A** and **B** go together with the first picture at the bottom, write **AB** in that picture's blank.

5. Rearrange the italicized word in this sentence to make a word that will fill in the blank.

> **He was *fretful* that he might gain weight if he ate even one more chocolate _____.**

6.

A	D	E	I	L	M	N	O	P	T
1	3	8	2	6	4	7	10	9	5

= 46   = ?

7. What Roman numeral completes this pattern?

> **_____, X, DL, C, MCL, DXV, I**

8. Each of the six letters below stands for one of the numbers from one to nine, and no letter stands for the same number as another letter. Using the four clues, can you deduce the number represented by each letter?

A	B	C
D	E	F

Clues: A is the largest number in the top row across.
The value of E is 9.
Each row across totals 12.
The middle column down totals twice the value of either of the two outside columns.

9. Word Ladder: Change **SOWS** to **OINK**, one letter at a time, in four steps. You must have a word at each step.

S O W S

— — — —

— — — —

— — — —

O I N K

10. Fill in a letter to complete a six-letter word reading either clockwise or counterclockwise. What is the word?

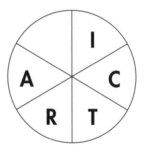

11. What number gives the same amount when it is added to 3 as when it is multiplied by 3?

12. What are the next two numbers in this sequence?

697   690   345   338   169   162   81   74   37   30   15

                                             __ __

13. What common English word contains the consecutive letter sequence XOP?

14. Here's a good one for crossword fans. Complete each set of blanks to make two common English words.

    _ P _ R _ A _ H   _ M _ R _ L _ A

15. Remove the first letter from the answer to the first clue to get the answer to the second clue. The four letters removed spell a word. What is the word?

A. Mountaineer / supple and lithe
B. Stature / number of sides on a stop sign
C. Fruit with a navel / cannon's distance
D. Drain fixer / cut wood

TEST 3

✦✦✦

1. Circle one letter in each word below that can be changed to another letter to make a new word. You must use the same replacement letter in each word. The letters you circle form a five-letter word. Use the same replacement letter with this word to make a final five-letter word. What's the final word?

CHEAT

LATER

OPINE

CLONE

PUREE

2. If the stack of blocks pictured here looks the same from all four directions, what is the maximum number of blocks that could be used to build it, based on what you can see from this angle?

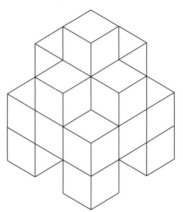

3. Put the same pair of letters in both blanks to make a word. (For example, __ __ **S E** __ __ **L L** becomes **BASEBALL**.)

__ __ **T R** __ __ **C H**

__ __ **S T** __ __ **N E**

__ __ **M A** __ __ **E S**

__ __ **T A** __ __ **A N**

4. Fran scored 76 on her first three tests of the year. What would she have to score on the fourth test to have an average of 81 on these four tests?

5. Rise to the challenge: What is the next word in this sequence?

STARE, ASSET, TASTE, SAUTE, STAVE, WASTE, TAXES, _____

6. Insert antonyms into the blanks to make two new words.

C _ _ _ _ A U   G _ _ _ _

7. Match each picture in the top row with a picture in the bottom row by writing the corresponding letter in the blank.

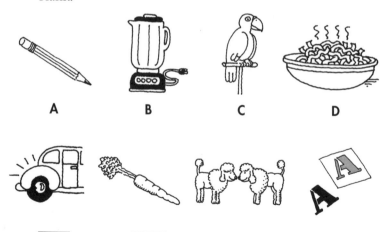

A   B   C   D

___   ___   ___   ___

8. What seven-letter word completes this analogy?

RIFFING is to GRIFFIN as ELATING is to _____

9. What letter comes next?

X   W   U   R   N   I   __

10. What type of pipe can be represented by LEAFLET in a cryptogram?

11. Solve these anagrams with the help of the pictures.

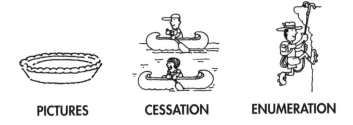

PICTURES   CESSATION   ENUMERATION

12. Get your calculator! If an EGGSHELL amounts to 77345663, then what vehicle is worth 461375?

13. What number completes the last diagram?

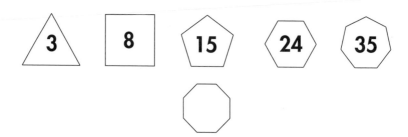

14. Fill in the letters to make a common *one-syllable* word.

_ _ _ E E _ _ E _

15. What number completes the last diagram?

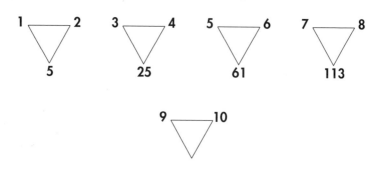

TEST 4

✦✦✦

1. The three underlined words are planets in our solar system. What is the answer to the question?

PK <u>STALK</u>, <u>JULIE</u>, EX <u>TOXIC</u> BOXICTKI BXER ICT KLA?

2. Unscramble the topic and the list.

Topic: MINALAS

SHORE

KESAN

MALEC

BRAZE

CONOCAR

NIPPOCURE

LOMALAIRD

3. Homophone pairs: If the principal hair on a horse's neck is the MAIN MANE, then what would you call a more disgusting supermarket owner?

4. Think of a word for the first blank, and remove one letter from the end to form the word for the second blank. What are the two words?

I threw out all of the _____ items around the tailor's shop, such as bent pins and _____.

5. What is the next term in this sequence?

4   11   32   95   284   851   2552   _____

6. Fill in a letter to complete a six-letter word reading either clockwise or counterclockwise. What is the word?

7. Add two lines to make this a true equation.

$$6 \quad 2 \quad = \quad 9 \quad 3$$

8. The Darts Players Association wants the phone number 782-4263 because of the seven-letter phrase the number spells. What's the phrase?

9. The dots in this grid are one unit apart horizontally and vertically. Find the area of the outlined region.

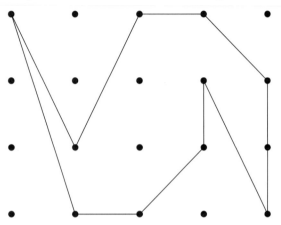

10. The same three-letter word can be inserted into all three words to form longer words. What word gets inserted?

R I _ _ _ N G   _ _ _ F F   O I L _ _ _ N

11. What single letter can be inserted into each of these words to form three new words?

PAIN   MUCH   MANY

12. A computer prints all of the numbers from 1 to 3456. How many times does it print the digit 5?

13. What 15-letter word is represented in our unusual country code?

Cuba Yip! Norway Greece Russia Vip! Turkey Zip! Laos Vip! Tunisia Xip! Yip! Nigeria Spain

14. Add the same letter six times (and appropriate spacing) to this string of letters to form four related words. You don't need to rearrange the letters in the string.

W O L G I R A E B U A L O E R R E T

15. The numbers in the diagrams combine in the same way to make correct arithmetic statements. What number is missing from the last diagram?

3	6
4	2

3	9
6	2

4	8
6	3

8	6
9	

TEST 5

1. Some years look the same right-side-up as upside-down.
   Find an example of such a year in the 19th century.

2. Which of **A**, **B**, or **C** belongs in the empty box at the end of
   the six-box series?

            A   **B**   **C**

3. Think of three words meaning "abandon" that also fit these definitions:

A. Purplish-red

B. Wasteland

C. Piece of yarn

4. Rhyme time! If the queen's long-eared hound is a REGAL BEAGLE, then what would you call only one shiver of excitement?

5. Which of the three choices, **A**, **B**, or **C**, goes with OCCUPATION so that it fits our matching scheme?

CLEVELAND & flat
ASTROPHYSICS & prize
LIFELINES & cat
ARCHIMEDES & rang
OCCUPATION & _____

A. deck   B. dock   C. duck

6. On each line, two six-letter words are woven together in order from left to right. Can you figure out the two words in each case?

VIPOURLEPTLE
BSIUZTZLTEER
SWINUTMERMER

7. 3F Y33 C3N F3G3R3 TH3S 33T, Y33 C3N 3GN3R3 V3W3LS!

8. Word Ladder: Can you change **HATE** to **LOVE**, one letter at a time, in four steps? You must have a word at each step.

H A T E

— — — —

— — — —

— — — —

L O V E

9. Give the fifth and sixth in this familiar sequence:

ST   ND   RD   TH   ___   ___

10. Fill in a letter to complete a six-letter word reading either clockwise or counterclockwise. What is the word?

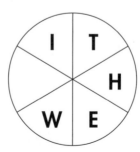

11. Think of a word for the first blank, and change one letter to form the word for the second blank. What are the two words?

Picking and eating Golden _____ apples
made me _____ with joy.

12. Insert a five-letter fruit, one letter per square, across the third row of this grid so that five common four-letter words are formed reading down.

O	C	T	A	L
W	H	I	T	E
S	W	E	P	T

13. What is the next term in this sequence?

Q1   P2   R6   N24   V120   _____

14. Match the items on the left with those on the right.

A. Personal automobile	___ redone
B. Demonstrator	___ yellow
C. Jokester	___ carmine
D. Show pain	___ pungent
E. Blusher	___ shower

15. Fill in the two letters in each pair to make words that rhyme.

Example: **C R A <u>N E</u>**   **T R A <u>I N</u>**

TOU _ _   SCU _ _

STE _ _   WHI _ _

PAS _ _   WAI _ _

TEST 6

1. Every letter in this 5 × 5 word square has been replaced by the same number everywhere it appears. Can you reconstruct the square with the help of the definitions? The definitions are not in the order of the words in the grid.

1	2	3	4	5
2	6	7	8	4
8	9	4	9	8
4	10	7	4	2
5	2	5	5	12

Floats, as through the air   Pert
Greek letter   Runs
Hawaiian hello   Skin blemishes
Homeless dog   Turning part
Parties   Warning

2. What single letter can be inserted into each of these words to form three new words?

RAID   SEAR   COOT

3. What word is represented by these words?

see are why pea tea eye sea

4. What is the next number in this sequence?

5   6   10   17   27   40   56   75   ____

5. The definitions in each row define three words. To get the next word, rearrange the last one with an F.

For example: BALE/FABLE/BAFFLE

A. Take a chair, clenched hand, rigid
B. Uses a bat, move slightly, certain fractions
C. Employs, angler, county officer

6. Each of the words below is misspelled. If the word is missing a letter or has an extra letter, write that letter in the blank. If a letter must be changed, write the correct letter in the blank. The letters in the blanks will form someone who needs good spelling.

mocasin   ___
violincello   ___
pavillion   ___
gutteral   ___
accomodate   ___
innoculate   ___
ideosyncrasy   ___
concensus   ___
diletante   ___

7. We've removed all of the letters in the word PROVERB anywhere they appear in a well-known four-word saying. The leftover letters are in the correct order. Can you reconstruct the wise words?

L K F Y U L A

8. Rearrange the italicized word in this sentence to make a word that will fill in the blank.

Society *matrons* tossed their unsolicited manuscripts over the

_____.

9. Insert antonyms into the blanks to make two new words.

C _ _ _ _ T   T _ _ _ G E

10. Match each seven-letter chunk in the first column with one in the second column so that you can remove a three-letter word from each to form a six-letter word or phrase, leaving an eight-letter word that's related. For example, **BETEAVE** and **RABAGGE** would go together to give **TEABAG** and **BEVERAGE**.

INFAIRL	**ARODNIC**
AJETFFL	**ABEDTED**
OUOLDTD	**UALPIES**
MECHOTH	**USETENT**
VIPOTCT	**ATHATED**

11. Which of the following, under the correct circumstances, could be Bob's father's sister's sister-in-law? (Choose as many as may apply.)

(a) Bob's mother   (b) Bob's wife   (c) Bob's daughter

12. Each of the six letters stands for one of the numbers one through six, and no letter stands for the same number as another letter. Using the three clues, can you deduce the number represented by each letter?

A	B	C
D	E	F

$(B \times B) + B = A$

$A + C + E = 14$

C, D, E, F are in decreasing order.

13. Match each picture in the top row with a picture in the bottom row by writing the corresponding letter in the blank.

A   **B**   **C**   **D**

____   ____   ____   ____

14. There are 360° in a circle. Through how many degrees does the minute hand of a clock turn in the time interval from 9:34 A.M. to 10:02 A.M. on the same morning?

15. Insert the 14 letters **C C L L N N P P R R V V Y Y** into the 14 blanks to form five words reading across.

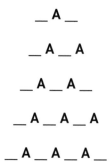

_ A _

_ A _ A

_ A _ A _

_ A _ A _ A

_ A _ A _ A _

TEST 7

1. What are the next two letters?

S E M I T M W Q T U F _ _

2. The numbers in the diagrams combine in the same way to make correct arithmetic statements. What number is missing from the last diagram?

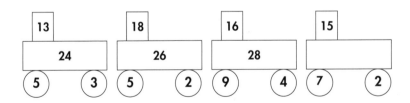

3. We've taken three related words and changed one letter in each. What were the original three words?

LAUGHTER   PIECE   BROTHEL

4. If this clock is turned upside down and held in front of a mirror, what time is reflected?

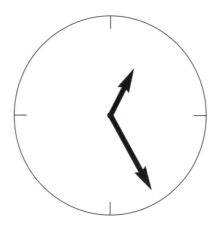

5. What number goes in the blank?

9, 61, 52, 63, 94, ____, 18

6. Place the jigsaw pieces into the tray to make five words reading across and five different words reading down. The pieces fit together with no overlap.

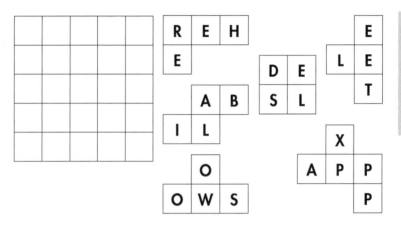

7. How's your code-breaking ability?

8. Find the eleven numbers from **ZERO** to **TEN** in this grid. Each word is in a straight line horizontally, vertically, or diagonally. The leftover letters spell a bonus word. What is this word?

O	C	Z	O	T	T
E	N	U	E	H	R
N	N	E	G	R	U
T	F	I	V	E	O
N	E	T	N	E	F
O	W	T	X	I	S

9. Think of a word for the first blank, and write its homophone in the second blank. What are the two words?

I _____ not be happy if you were to burn

all of the chopped _____ in tonight's fire.

10. What single letter can be inserted into each of these words to form three new words?

BRED

BORN

FLAT

11. Add the same letter eight times (and appropriate spacing) to this string of letters to form four related words. You don't need to rearrange the letters in the string.

R O N O D N E R D U M L T H U M

12. Fill in a letter to complete a six-letter word reading either clockwise or counterclockwise. What is the word?

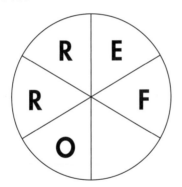

13. A pencil and eraser together cost $2.60. The eraser costs $2.00 more than the pencil. How much does the pencil cost?

14. This is a list of eight six-letter birds in a simple substitution code. Can you crack the code and identify the birds?

HNGBNZ	HSHPNN
DMKHNG	UMYFLI
NZLNKI	FLYING
ANSHMG	ASZPIR

15. Fill in the blanks to form two different common words.

__ __ __ A N S E   __ __ __ A N S E

TEST 8

1. Place the eight tiles into the grid so that four six-letter words are formed, two reading across and two reading down.

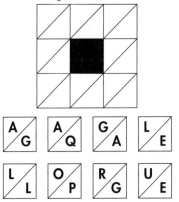

2. Move one digit to make this equation true:

1 2 2 = 1 4 4

3. Circle one letter in each word below that can be changed to another letter to make a new word. You must use the same replacement letter in each word. The letters you circle form a five-letter word. Use the same replacement letter with this word to make a final five-letter word. What's the final word?

AFTER

REPAY

DAILY

GRAIN

STING

4. Which anagram is the odd one out?

SOLO   PAIRS   LOUSE   ANIMAL   ENEMY   QUOIT

5. How many times does the word **YES** appear in this grid in a straight line horizontally, vertically, or diagonally?

Y	S	Y	S	Y
Y	E	E	E	S
E	Y	S	Y	E
S	E	Y	E	S
Y	E	S	E	Y

6. Find two different ways to make 24 using one digit three times and as many + signs as you need (but no other operation symbols). The digit isn't the same in the two different ways.

7. This word search in reverse should be as easy as ABC. Place the 13 words into the grid in straight lines horizontally, vertically, and diagonally. We've already placed all of the **A**'s, **B**'s, and **C**'s as guides. When you've filled the grid, find a bonus seven-letter word created by the words you entered.

ACQUITS
ALLOW
ARIAS
ASCRIBE
BISQUE
BLAB
BUBBLE
MAIZE
QUENCH
QUILT
SPATTER
SCROLL
WATER

					B	
B						
			A			A
		B				
C			B			
	C					
A			A			

8. At this round table of males (M) and females (F), the number of people sitting next to a female is _____ and the number of people sitting next to a male is _____.

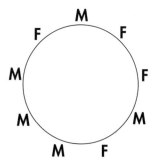

9. What letter in this grid is being described by the statement below the grid?

The letter directly below the letter exactly between the letter just left of the letter two below G and the letter just below the letter to the right of B.

10. Match each picture in the top row with a picture in the bottom row by writing the corresponding letter in the blank.

11. Unlike Joe, I was lying when I denied arguing against scrapping the proposal. Was Joe in favor of or against the proposal?

12. Lockers in a high school hallway are numbered consecutively from 678 to 789. How many lockers are in the hallway?

13. WABBYT HAT WBOOTWH CRYPTO:

C.   ZBR'H HCLT ET

X.   G'E SOBXCXDI RBH GH

W.   YTDTWH Z GRYHTCZ

Z.   PGRRTO'Y SGWL

14. What four-letter word completes this analogy?

PERFORM is to PROM as COLLUDE is to _____

15. What letter/number combination goes in the blank?

A4   B6   C2   D9   E8   L7   M5   R3   ____

TEST 9

◆◆◆

1. Here are four views of the same block. Draw the correct front face on the final block.

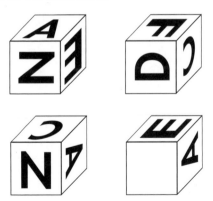

2. What word meaning "foe" can be represented by FOOFARAW in a cryptogram?

3. Word Ladder: Change **LADY** to **MISS**, one letter at a time, in four steps. You must have a word at each step.

L   A   D   Y

—   —   —   —

—   —   —   —

—   —   —   —

M   I   S   S

4. Every row and column of this grid contains the letters **A**, **B**, and **C** once each. Deduce the contents of the grid using the letters outside the grid as clues. Each exterior letter tells you the first letter you encounter in the grid when you enter the grid from that point. For example, in the second column from the left, the first letter is a B, but it may or may not be in the top square.

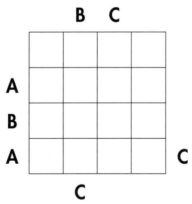

5. Insert antonyms into the blanks to make two new words.

_ _ _ _ _ **T T O**   **M I S C O N S** _ _ _ _

6. This year, I made $165 at my yard sale, which is an increase of 10% over last year. How much did I make last year?

7. What playing card comes next?

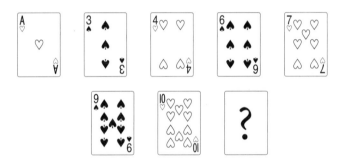

8. What anagram of MOONSTARERS is a group of people who might be described as "moon starers"?

9. Mentally transfer the nine pieces into the grid in the appropriate places. What picture appears?

	A	B	C
1			
2			
3			

C3   B3   A3

C2   B2   A2

C1   B1   A1

10. Fill in a letter to complete a six-letter word reading either clockwise or counterclockwise. What is the word?

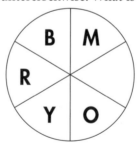

11. The average of the ages of the five people in a room is 30. A sixth person joins the room and the average age rises to 32. How old is the sixth person?

12. Go from **FORMER** to **LATTER** in this word maze. The last two letters of one word are the first two letters of the next. Not every word will be used. What is the correct path of words?

CYCLIC	ICEBOX	NEATEN	SERAPH
DELUDE	IDIOCY	NEBULA	TACKLE
ENIGMA	IODINE	ONSIDE	TAUNTS
EROTIC	LATTER*	OXYGEN	THWART
ERRATA	LENGTH	PHOTON	TSETSE
*FORMER	MADRID	PHYSIO	

13. Use these three words to make a phrase meaning "officially."

FORT   HERE   CORD

14. SHOWER TEST can be rearranged to make the two words SHORT & SWEET. Rearrange these letters to make a different pair of "this & that" words.

KIND OF ROD

15. Think of a word for the first blank, and remove its first letter to form the word for the second blank. What are the two words?

The _____ of the United States is the most

famous _____ of the White House.

TEST 10

1. Remove three letters from DISPARAGE and rearrange the others to form an antonym of disparage.

2. Find the next three terms of this sequence:

128 61 Y 64 63 S 32 65 N 16 67 J 8 69 G __ __ __

3. Can you rearrange the chess pieces so that this makes more sense?

4. The diagram below is made of eight squares, all the same size. The perimeter of (distance around) any one of the squares is 100 inches. What is the perimeter of the entire shape, in inches?

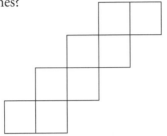

5. What five-letter card game becomes a card when you change its first letter?

6. The numbers in the diagrams combine in the same way to make correct arithmetic statements. What number is missing from the last diagram?

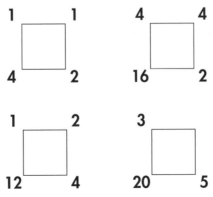

7. Rhyme time! If a dumb symbol of love is a STUPID CUPID, what would you call a person who damages a birthday cake topper?

8. On a balance scale, the following have equal weights:

   2 chocolate chunks = 20 jellybeans

   15 jellybeans = 6 licorice sticks

   How many chocolate chunks are needed to balance 20 licorice sticks?

9. What five-letter word completes this analogy?

   ASPARAGUS is to SUGAR as TRAGIC is to _____

10. Rearrange the italicized word in this sentence to make a word that will fill in the blank.

    He *claimed* his _____ expenses after his accident.

11. How should the last triangle be labeled?

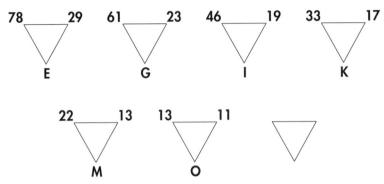

12. What single letter can be inserted into each of these words to form three new words?

GAZE   ONCE   PROD

13. We've assigned different whole numbers to letters and then multiplied their values together to make the values of words. For example, if F = 5, O = 3 and X = 2, then FOX = 30.

Given that:

TEEN = 52

TILT = 77

TALL = 363

What's the value of TATTLE?

14. Add the same letter six times (and appropriate spacing) to this string of letters to form four related words. You don't need to rearrange the letters in the string.

T P A Z M N S T N E P A L N Y X

15. Fill in the final number.

ZOOLOGIST	=	4443
INITIATOR	=	33314
WATERSHED	=	122
BEEKEEPER	=	22222
SUCCULENT	=	552
EDUCATION	=	_____

TEST 11

1. Reconstruct this familiar warning.

YAP THE REC PEA ORA LOS IRR INM HAN ERT CTS BJE

O _ _ _ _ _ _ _ _ _ _ _ _ _ _ _ _ _ _ _ _ _ _ _ _ _ _ _ _ _ _ _ _ _ _ _ _ R

2. Tom drove away from Bigtown 10 minutes after Janice, and overtook her in 20 minutes. If Tom drove at a speed of 90 mph, what was Janice's speed in mph?

3. Match each picture in the top row with a picture in the bottom row by writing the corresponding letter in the blank.

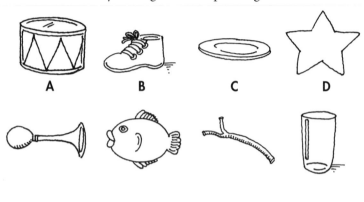

A   B   C   D

____   ____   ____   ____

4. The names of three world countries have been written in a row without spaces and with the vowels removed. What are the three countries?

S   T   R   S   T   N   N   G   L

5. Place the eight tiles into the grid so that four six-letter words are formed, two reading across and two reading down.

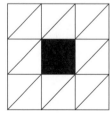

6. What is the next term in this sequence?

2   9   11   20   31   51   82   133   ____

7. Change one letter in each of these two words to make a familiar saying.

HONEY TANKS

8. In chemistry, if you were to combine tungsten, iodine, sulphur, carbon, oxygen, and nitrogen with sulphur, iodine, and nitrogen, in what state would the result be?

9. Circle one letter in each word below that can be changed to another letter to make a new word. You must use the same replacement letter in each word. The letters you circle form a five-letter word. Use the same replacement letter with this word to make a final five-letter word. What's the final word?

**ALLOT
ROUND
AIRED
DRAIN
SLING**

10. Among them, three children have 75 marbles. Jane has five times as many marbles as Paul, and Sam has five more marbles than Paul. How many marbles does Paul have?

11. Ball A moves counterclockwise, one position at a time.

If ball A lands on a shaded area, ball B moves two places
counterclockwise.

If ball A lands on an unshaded area, ball B moves one place
clockwise.

If ball B lands on a shaded area, ball C moves three places
clockwise.

If ball B lands on an unshaded area, ball C moves one place
counterclockwise.

Over the next six moves of ball A, what six-letter word is
spelled out by ball C?

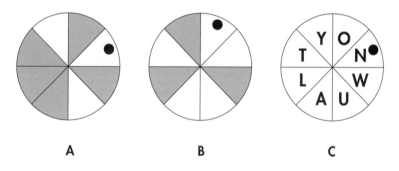

A   B   C

12. Circle six different letters in the alphabet below to make a
cotton fabric reading from left to right.

A B C D E F G H I J K L M N O P Q R S T U V W X Y Z

13. A $6 \times 6 \times 6$ cube is formed by gluing together 216 wooden blocks that are $1 \times 1 \times 1$. If the cube is resting on a table, what is the maximum number of $1 \times 1 \times 1$ blocks that you can see from any angle at any one time? (If you can see even one face of a $1 \times 1 \times 1$ block, then count it.)

14. Replace the blanks in the first word with two letters, and then reverse the order of the two letters and put them in the blanks of the second word.

Example: **M A C H O   M O C H A**

Q U I _ _   Q U I _ _

_ L O _ T   _ L O _ T

B U _ _ E   B U _ _ E

15. Fill in a letter to complete a six-letter word reading either clockwise or counterclockwise. What is the word?

TEST 12

◆ ◆ ◆

1. Match each picture in the top row with a picture in the bottom row by writing the corresponding letter in the blank.

A   B   C   D

____   ____   ____   ____

2. Rhyme time! What might a rhymer call clam soup mix?

3. Complete the eight words using the clues, which are presented in scrambled order. The words filled into the blanks will spell some advice.

T __ __ F	Hot dog topping
J O __ __ __ S	Take as one's own
__ __ __ __ A R D	House
E N __ __ W	Happy; jubilant
D __ __ C H	Hotel room
A __ __ P T	Roadside excavation
S U __ __ E	Minor argument
D __ __ __ __ I N G	Furnish

4. A palindrome is a number that reads the same when its digits are reversed. For example, 2552 and 30903 are palindromes. How many palindromes are there between 700 and 1700?

5. Match each word in the top row with a picture in the bottom row by writing letters in the blanks. One of the four pictures provides a slight hint.

main ___   **ours** ___   **four** ___   **pain** ___

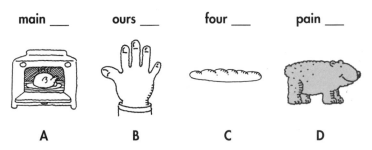

A   B   C   D

6. Kathy begins with her game token on the square marked START and moves clockwise around the board. Each turn she moves the token one more square than the number of squares she moved on the previous turn. On her first turn, she moves one square; on her second turn, she moves two squares; on her third turn, she moves three squares; and so on. On which turn does Kathy first land back on START?

START			

7. Insert antonyms into the blanks to make two new words.

_ _ _ _ D Y   B I _ _ T

8. Think of a word for the first blank, and remove the last two letters to form the word for the second blank. What are the two words?

By not asking visitors to remove their shoes,

Bob and Jill essentially _____ the tracking of

mud throughout their third-floor _____.

9. What is the next term in this sequence?

101   97   91   83   73   61   47   ___

10. Seven different letters that touch each other on a typewriter keyboard can be *rearranged* to spell a seven-letter, two-word cutting tool. (You will need to rearrange the seven letters; the answer cannot be spelled out by moving consecutively from key to key.) What is this tool?

11. What five-letter word completes this analogy?

RAPSCALLION is to RASCAL

as

COMPADRES is to _____

12. Dave buys $200 worth of paint and Sue buys $40 worth of paintbrushes. If they want to split costs equally, how much money does Sue owe Dave?

13. Which anagram is the odd one out?

OREAD

HESRICH

JONEY

BROAH

ZEILOID

14. Each of the four symbols in this grid represents a different
number. Seven of the row and column totals are given.
What is the total of the last column?

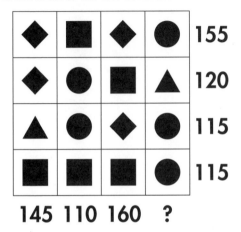

155
120
115
115

145 110 160   ?

15. What single letter can be inserted into each of these words
to form three new words?

EASE

LEAN

MOON

TEST 13

1. If today is Sunday, what day of the week will it be 4400 days from today?

2. What letter logically fills in the empty space?

E F M U P L T L __

3. Five teams are in a huge round robin tournament in which every team plays every other team three times. How many games take place?

4. On this dartboard, how many numbers are in the longest string of prime numbers that appear consecutively along the edge?

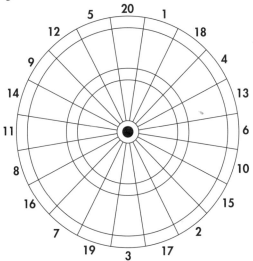

5. This is a list of nine six-letter chemical elements in a simple substitution code. Can you crack the code and identify the elements?

MTOWRU	AIXXYO	IBPLYC
ATOMIC	WIFWCY	QWEJYO
AIMTES	CWANYE	QIFWRU

6. Fill in a letter to complete a six-letter word reading either clockwise or counterclockwise. What is the word?

7. Match each word in the top row with a picture in the bottom row by writing letters in the blanks.

mare ___   crow ___   writer ___   fool ___

A   B   C   D

8. Insert a five-letter weapon (that is useless by itself) across the second row of this grid so that five common four-letter words are formed reading down.

B	O	O	Z	E
S	C	E	N	E
E	A	S	E	S

9. The numbers in the diagrams combine in the same way to make correct arithmetic statements. What number is missing from the last diagram?

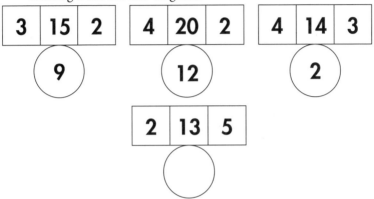

10. What is the next term in this sequence?

32   48   72   108   162   ___

11. In each line, find a word that follows the first word and precedes the second word to form two phrases (such as **SECOND** ___ ___ ___ ___ ___ ___ **SPLIT** making "second banana" and "banana split" when **BANANA** is entered.) The three words you supply, in order, will form a familiar phrase.

PLASTER	___ ___ ___ ___	**ANCHOR**
STEAM	___ ___ ___ ___	**MAIDEN**
WEAK	___ ___ ___ ___ ___ ___	**FLU**

IQ TESTERS
Test 13

12. Which is the odd one out?

13. Given that the key for this domino code is AEGLMNR, what two-word job does it spell?

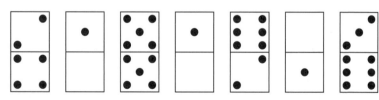

14. Rearrange these three-letter chunks to make a proverb. You don't have to change the order of the letters in any of the chunks.

AKE   HAS   STE   SWA   TEM

15. Add the same letter seven times (and appropriate spacing) to this string of letters to form four related words. You don't need to rearrange the letters in the string.

C I A M O C U M I G I G E R F E E L

TEST 14

1. Rearrange the italicized word in this sentence to make a word that will fill in the blank.

The doctor _____ the *educator* and the lawyer in the marathon.

2. The sum of the digits of the square of a one-digit number is 6 more than the number. What is the one-digit number?

3. Name a sport that is also a vegetable. _____

   Name a sport that is also an insect. _____

   Name a sport that is also an explorer. _____

4. An evening theater performance is scheduled every third day. What is the maximum number of performances that can take place over a 25-day period?

5. What three-letter chunk completes this set?

URY   NUS   RTH   ARS   TER   URN   NUS   UNE   ___

6. The same three-letter word can be inserted into all three blanks to form longer words. What word gets inserted?

D R __ __ __ R   S E __ __ __ E D   O U T L __ __ __ D

7. Change one letter in each of the following words to make a familiar saying.

OFT IF TIGHT, BUT ON MINK

8. What six-letter word completes this analogy?

TIMBERLINE is to GERMANY as COMPARISON is to _____

9. Change one letter in each of these four words and then respace the result without rearranging the chunks to make a familiar piece of advice.

DOGS   ISAR   NOVA   SIDE

10. Match two of the lettered pictures with each picture in the bottom row by writing their two letters in the blank. For example, if pictures **A** and **B** went together with the first picture at the bottom, you'd write **AB** in that picture's blank.

A   B   C   D

E   F   G   H

____   ____   ____   ____

11. What is the next term in this sequence?

216   108   36   9   1.8   ____

12. Wing has nine tasks—P, Q, R, S, T, U, V, W, and X—that he'd like to do over the months October to February, and he plans to do two tasks every month except December. In December, he does only one task.

He does S in November and W in February.
He does R three months after he does T.
He does V and X in the same month.
He does U in a month before the month he does P.
He does V in a month after the month that he does Q.

Which two tasks does Wing do in October?

13. What single letter can be inserted into each of these words to form three new words?

TACT

MOST

PLOT

14. Enter the answers to the clues radially inward, one letter per space. The last letters of the words, already entered, will help you place the four-letter answers, which are clued in no particular order. When you're finished, the shaded area will spell a two-word phrase that you'll be lucky to get.

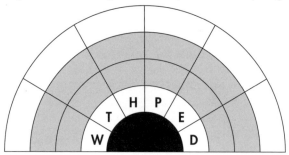

Clues
Cover a birthday gift
Sunrise direction
Had debts
Curved masonry construction
Faith, _____, charity
Was aware of

15. A company has 21 employees consisting of regular workers, vice presidents, and one president. All of the employees chip in money for a charity drive. Regular workers pay $7 each, vice presidents pay $17 each, and the president pays $30. If the company collects $200 in all, how many regular employees are there?

TEST 15

1. Match each expression below with one of the lettered pictures.

___ put out to sea
___ fits like a glove
___ based on a true story
___ have a nice day
___ like it or not

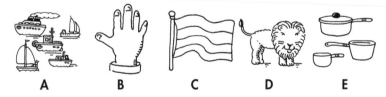

A **B** **C** **D** **E**

2. AHW EVES-ETTEL ROW NINAEM "SENISUB TAICOSSA"
LIW MOCEB EHTONA ROW NINAEM "RUTPAC" EHW
OY VOMER TI ANIF ETTEL NA RUT I RAWKCAB?

3. The same pair of letters can be inserted side by side into each of these four words, forming a new word each time. What pair of letters is it?

DIVER
PRUDE
GRAVY
TANGO

4. Place the eight tiles into the grid so that four six-letter words are formed, two reading across and two reading down.

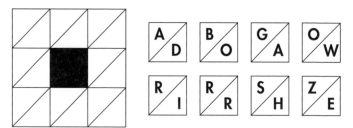

5. The houses on one side of a street are numbered with consecutive *even* numbers. If the house numbers start at 28 and end at 130, how many houses are there on this side of the street?

6. Insert antonyms into the blanks to make two new words.

ORC _ _ _ _   QU _ _ _ _

7. A six-card shuffling machine always rearranges the six cards in its hopper in the same way every time you press its button. The cards in the hopper start out in this order:

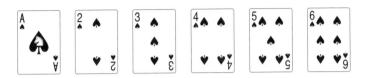

After one push of the button, the cards are in this order:

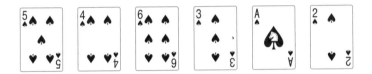

What is the fewest number of times you must now push the button to get the cards back into their original consecutive order?

8. OTHER STEWS can be rearranged to make the two words SHORT & SWEET. Rearrange these letters to make a different pair of "this & that" words.

EMERALD FITS

9. Fill in a letter to complete a six-letter word reading either clockwise or counterclockwise. What is the word?

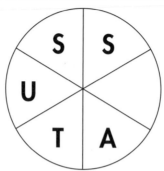

10. How many numbers between 1 and 1000 have the property that the sum of their digits is equal to 3?

11. What anagram of COBRA gives you the selections you might expect on a multiple-choice test?

12. What sport can be represented by NEATNESS in a cryptogram?

13.

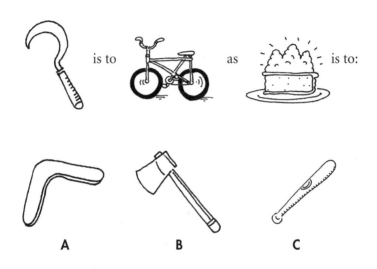

is to

as

is to:

A   B   C

14. What are the next two terms in this sequence?

4438   4440   1110   1112   278

280   70   72   18   ___   ___

15.

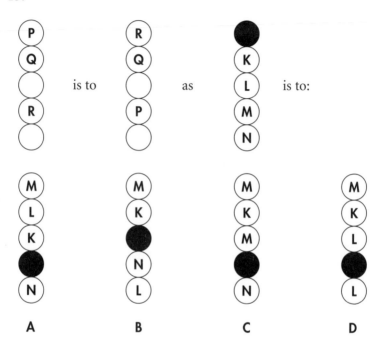

TEST 16

◆ ◆ ◆

1. Robin shoots three arrows that all hit this target, and he attains a score of 13. How many different combinations give a sum of 13?

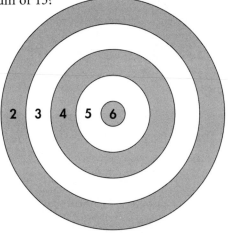

2. What is the next term in this sequence?

371   370   367   358   331   250   ____

3. Rearrange the words on the left to match the clues on the right, then enter the letters across, one letter per space. The shaded columns will spell something appropriate.

MARES						Use finger paints
FLIER						Hunter's gun
LATEX						Praise
EQUIP						Irritate
POSTS						Doesn't continue

4. If L. B. at F. means "life begins at forty," then what familiar saying is this?

B. L. than N.

(To which one may respond, using the same words: B. N. L.!)

5. Two six-letter words are coded in this letter grid. Each number in the code represents the sum of column and row headings of that letter. Each letter in the grid is used exactly once, so it's a good idea to cross off each one as you use it. What are the two coded words?

	1	**2**	**3**	**4**
1	M	O	R	E
2	T	H	A	N
3	E	V	E	R

Word A: 4 4 5 5 6 6

Word B: 3 7 5 2 3 4

6. What single letter can be inserted into each of these words to form three new words?

SAME   LATE   USER

7. What appendage is represented here?

THETA   ILO   FAMOUS   E

8. Janice has five different pins and wants to choose two to wear with her outfit today. How many different combinations of two pins can she pick?

9. Add the same letter seven times (and appropriate spacing) to this string of letters to form four related words. You don't need to rearrange the letters in the string.

O O A O G N A O F F E E U R A A O

10. The four underlined words are all compass points. What is the answer to the question?

HLOIL AX <u>CAMEL</u>, <u>GAVEL</u>, <u>URGE</u>, AM <u>HUGE</u>

OG "VW" AC PAGE PRWG?

11. Add one line to make a true equation. You may not change the equals sign.

6 I I = 7

12. Which is the odd one out?

13. This is a list of eight six-letter islands in a simple substitution code. Can you crack the code and identify the islands?

RXGGWE	MFEDMN
RFAEJF	DWIWZS
ISLAND	UXMWUW
MXBXWW	UXWBXE

14. Think of a word for the first blank, and remove the first three letters to form the word for the second blank. What are the two words?

By paying extra for a courier service, he _____ the delivery

of the carefully _____ manuscript.

15. The numbers in the diagrams combine in the same way to make correct arithmetic statements. What number is missing from the last diagram?

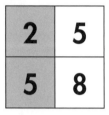

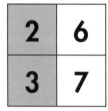

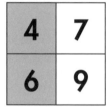

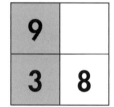

TEST 17

1. What one-word anagram of A CENT TIP might describe a cent tip?

2. Add the same letter twice to each word, making a new word. For example, given TALC, you could add two I's to make ITALIC. Write one copy of the letter you add into the blank. The blanks, when filled, spell something appropriate.

MILE	___
MINUS	___
SALLY	___
CLUED	___
WORDY	___
GLAND	___
WISER	___
VERGE	___
ICING	___
CLANS	___

199

3. I'm thinking of two phrases, each meaning "to date." They are both two-word phrases made up of a two-letter word followed by a three-letter word. What are the two phrases?

4. Match each picture in the top row with a picture in the bottom row by writing the corresponding letter in the blank.

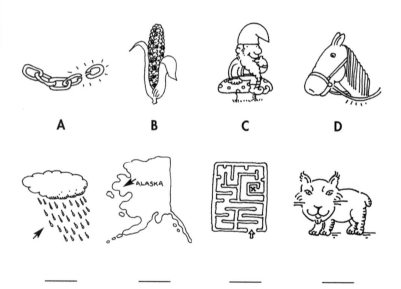

A   B   C   D

___   ___   ___   ___

5. What word completes this analogy?

ALOUD is to BARD as SYNCH is to _____

6. Rearrange these letters to make two words that are antonyms.

FOLDOUTS

7. Put the nine words, crossword-style, into this 5 × 5 grid. One letter has already been inserted for you. The shaded region will spell a five-letter word that does not appear in the word list. What is this word?

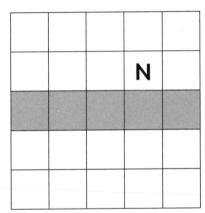

A L O H A
A L O N E
A N I S E
C H E S T
H A D E S
L AMA S
L A T C H
MO P E D
S E C T S

8. What common English word contains the consecutive letter sequence SPB?

9. What is the fewest number of blocks you need to add to make this shape into a cube?

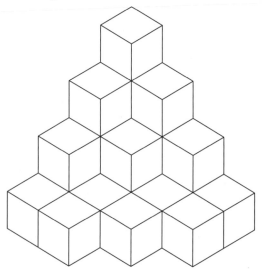

10. What number and letter go on the last domino?

2	O	5	O	12	O	23	
M	3	N	8	P	17	L	

11. What does this say?

NE   RC   PY   IT   NO

12. Circle one letter in each word below that can be changed to another letter to make a new word. You must use the same replacement letter in each word. The letters you circle form a five-letter word. Use the same replacement letter with this word to find a final five-letter word. What's the final word?

CHEST

PROSE

STREW

MEDIC

CHINK

13. Five people want a photographer to take pictures of every possible group of three of them. How many different photos will the photographer need to take?

14. Rearrange these three-letter chunks to make a saying. You don't have to change the order of the letters in any of the chunks.

ACA   ING   OKA   TAK   TMA   YLO

15. Fill in a letter to complete a six-letter word reading either clockwise or counterclockwise. What is the word?

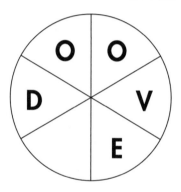

TEST 18

1. What single letter can be inserted into each of these words to form three new words?

JABS   THEE   ABLE

2. Insert antonyms into the blanks to make two new words.

U _ _ _ _ T H   S E A _ _ _ I N G

3. What is the next term in this math-based sequence?

23   21   24   19   26   15   28   11   30   7   36   ___

4. What number belongs below the last clock?

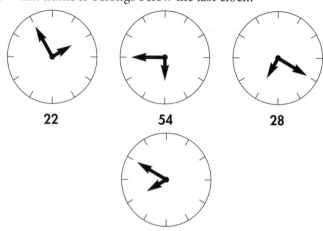

22   54   28

5. Rhyme Time! Find the odd one out, based on the category.

Category:

6. Change one letter in each word to form a familiar saying.

REVENUE IN SWEAT

7. Put the digits from 1 to 9, one per square, in this grid so that multiplying the numbers across and down give the column and row products shown outside the grid.

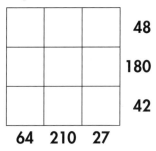

8. A bookcase is 208 cm high and has six shelves on which to rest books. The top of the bookcase (i.e., the plank above the top row of books) is the same width as any of the other five shelves in the bookcase. However, the bottom of the bookcase (on which the bottom row of books rests) includes a decorative base that puts the top surface of the bottom shelf 10 cm off the floor. If the shelves inside the bookcase are all 2 cm thick and the vertical distances between the bookshelves are all equal, what is the height, in cm, of the largest book that you can just fit, standing up, in this bookcase?

9. *I'm always ninth in tournaments;*
I'm third in contests, see?
I'm sixth in pageants, always sixth!
Now, what's the name for me?

10. Place the eight tiles into the grid so that four six-letter words are formed, two reading across and two reading down.

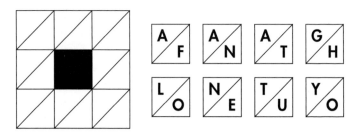

11. Fill in the blanks to make two different words that mean "catch."

_ R A _   _ R A _

12. Remove one letter at a time from the word below to make smaller and smaller words. No rearranging is allowed. Can you reduce the word to a single letter?

SPARKLING

13. Rearrange the italicized word in this sentence to make a word that will fill in the blank.

They were *hustling* to get the tent set up

before the _____ disappeared for the day.

14. Match each picture in the top row with a picture in the bottom row by writing the corresponding letter in the blank.

A   B   C   D

____   ____   ____   ____

15. Four rectangles, each measuring 5 units by 11 units, are
arranged as shown. What is the perimeter (distance around)
the entire shape?

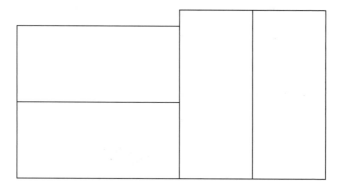

TEST 19

1. What number goes in the blank?

   823543   46656   3125   256   ___   4   1

2. What word meaning "ropes and chains on sailing vessels" can be represented by VESSELS in a cryptogram?

3. Join these fragments to form four nine-letter words.

                    ACK   GER
                    ARD   HOR
                    ATE   LEV
                    BOU   MES
                    CHE   SEB
                    CKM   SEN

IQ TESTERS
Test 19

211

4.

is to ⬛ as ⬛ is to:

A   B   C

5. Add the same letter six times (and appropriate spacing) to this string of letters to form four related words. You don't need to rearrange the letters in the string.

S D A N G A N D A R G A Y P E R

6. I'm convinced that even brisk solvers will require a few minutes to figure out which two letters just do not appear in this exciting sentence.

7. Fill in the only common word of the given length that comes alphabetically between each of the two given words in a dictionary.

DAEMON	PANPIPE	TUITION
__ __ __ __ __ __ __ __	__ __ __ __ __	__ __ __ __ __
DAFFY	PANT	TULLE

8. In each line, find a word that follows the first word and precedes the second word to form two phrases (such as **SECOND** __ __ __ __ __ __ **SPLIT** making "second banana" and "banana split" when **BANANA** is entered.) The three words you supply, in order, will form a familiar phrase.

EYES	__ __ __ __ __	DOOR
SKID	__ __ __	HOUSE
BICYCLE	__ __ __ __	BELT

9. Put these 10 three-letter groups in order so that each set of two adjacent groups forms a six-letter word.

BAL	TLE	LES	HER	SEX	NET	TET	SON	LAD	UNI

10. Which is the odd one out?

11. STREET SHOW can be rearranged to make the two words
SHORT & SWEET. Rearrange these letters to make a
different pair of "this & that" words.

FEAR US, IRAQ

12. The numbers in the diagrams combine in the same way to make correct arithmetic statements. What number is missing from the last diagram?

2	16
4	2

2	36
6	3

4	60
5	3

2	80
	8

13. What five-letter name completes this analogy?

DOLT is to GROW as COBRA is to _____

14. Fill in a letter to complete a six-letter word reading either clockwise or counterclockwise. What is the word?

15. What common ten-letter word contains the letters IZM next to each other?

TEST 20

1. Rhyme time! What would you call a grater that only grates a certain type of orange cheese?

2. Circle six different letters in the reverse alphabet below to make something that is full of holes and still holds water. The word reads from left to right.

Z Y X W V U T S R Q P O N M L K J I H G F E D C B A

3. Jerry has a set of 11 cards, each card numbered with a different number from 20 to 30 inclusive. He wants to select three cards whose sum is 75. How many such sets of three are possible if the card labeled 24 must be one of the cards Jerry chooses?

4. This octagonal wheel that turns clockwise has the letters A through H on consecutive faces, with letter D on the front face to start with. The wheel is turned first one position, then three positions, then five positions, then seven positions, then nine positions. What letter ends up on the front face?

5. In the 6/49 lottery, you choose six numbers from 1 to 49 inclusive and you win the grand prize if the six numbers selected in the draw match your six numbers. To check their ticket, a man gets a newspaper and reads to his wife the numbers that were chosen from the previous night's draw. But after he reads out only the first number, she lets out a cheer, knowing from that number alone that they've won. What was the number that the man read?

6. Put the seven three-letter tiles into the correct spaces to make a five-word truism. You must supply the breaks between the words in the final statement.

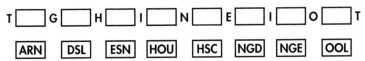

T [   ] G [   ] H [   ] I [   ] N [   ] E [   ] I [   ] O [   ] T

| ARN | DSL | ESN | HOU | HSC | NGD | NGE | OOL |

7. What single letter can be inserted into each of these words to form three new words?

AIDE   PRIM   HATE

8. Find the seven related words (unscramble the first one).

CDEMOY

D _ _ _ A

H _ _ _ _ R

M _ _ _ _ _ Y

R _ _ _ _ _ E

S _ _ - _ I

T _ _ _ _ _ _ R

9. Put the same three letters in both sets of blanks to make two words that mean "let out."

R _ _ _   V _ _ _

10. Using 1 = A, 2 = B, 3 = C, etc., decipher our playing-card coding scheme and decode the final word.

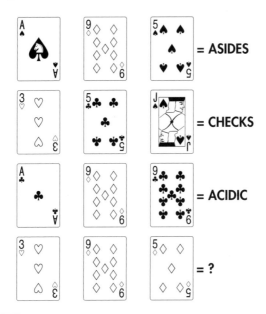

11. What is the next term in this sequence?

4   7   12   20   33   54   88   143   232   376   ____

12. Beginning with the color CARMINE, remove two consecutive letters and rearrange the rest to form another color.

13. The body parts eye, ear, leg, arm, and toe all have three letters. Come up with three other parts of the body consisting of only three letters. (No slang, please!)

14. Insert the three-word title of a Shakespeare play into the blanks to form three new words.

TES＿ ＿ ＿ ＿ ＿Y   S ＿ ＿ A   HE＿ ＿ ＿ ＿ ＿ ＿

15. From the choices given, which word completes the sentence?

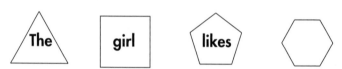

The choices are **candy, chocolate, sweets, popcorn,** or **licorice.**

ANSWERS

WARM UPS

Verbal Test 1

1. ADMIRE, REASON, ONSIDE, DEFILE, LENGTH, THREAD
2. Firing on all cylinders.
3. OBLITERATE, CREATE
4. ARTIFICE
5. LIKE FATHER LIKE SON
6. GRACIOUS, CORDIAL
7. BALL
8. ACACIA
9. BLUSHING
10. HOUSE
11. WIGGLE
12. SUGGESTIVE
13. WASHROOM
14. MAJESTIC, STRIKING
15. PAPUA NEW GUINEA

Verbal Test 2

1. LOQUACIOUS
2. END. ENDOWED, ENDEAR, ENDLESS, ENDLONG, ENDANGER.

3. MISCOMPREHENSION

4. ENCIPHER

5. GOWN. All the words in the left-hand column can now be prefixed with NIGHT and all the words in the right-hand column can now be prefixed with DAY.

6. NICHE, PLACE

7. Sell like hot cakes.

8. MALADROIT, DEXTROUS

9. CAPUCHIN

10. (c) CONVOCATION

11. MONKEY

12. FISH

13. Anyone who thinks there is some good in everyone hasn't interviewed enough people.

14. ORANGUTAN

15. PINNACLE

Verbal Test 3

1. NECESSARY, SUPERFLUOUS

2. PARTISAN, OPPONENT

3. (c) SALAMANDER

4. EVIL OLIVE

5. MICROWAVE

6. RIPE/PEAR, CODE/DEER, LAST/STAR, OVAL/ALLY.
Eight-letter word: PEDESTAL

7. RUDDER

8. (d) AFFIRMATION

9. CHIVES

10. SOUBRETTE

11. Society is threatened less by the fat around the middle than it is menaced by the fat between the ears.

12. DULLNESS, RADIANCE

13. They are all aquatic creatures: CARP, CRAB, DACE, CHUB, NEWT

14. BATHYSCOPE

15. FENCING, CRICKET

Verbal Test 4

1. SABTL = BLAST

2. BANAL

3. SCUBA DIVER

4. Chance favors the prepared mind.

5. RATIONAL, SENSIBLE

6. FAULTY, IMPERFECT

7. PLAUSIBLE

8. The world gets better every day then worse again in the evening.

9. OBSTINATE, DOGGED

10. (a) A SHELL

11. INVECTIVE, SECRETION

12. (e) WHITE

13. MEDIOCRE, ORDINARY

14. PUSSYCAT

15. UMBRELLA

Verbal Test 5

1. CONSORT
2. C(HERO)KEE
3. GRATE
4. XYZ = TOP. TOPPLE, UTOPIA, ESTOPS, LAPTOP
5. ROCHESTER: FIR, TOO, ARC, ASH, PIE, WAS, PAT, RUE, BAR
6. EMERALD, AMETHYST, TOPAZ
7. BREAD, PIZZA, STEAK, BACON, HONEY
8. SECOND
9. TREADMILL
10. FLOUNDER
11. ASSASSINS
12. IMPUDENT, CONTRARY
13. WHIRLWINDS
14. Once you can open a can of worms, the only way to recan them is to use a longer can.
15. CANDLEWICK

Visual Test 1

1. D. The figure rotates 90° clockwise at each stage and a different section is shaded in turn.
2. E. Triangles turn to circles and vice versa, and white figures turn to black and vice versa.
3. E. In all the others, the triangle is in the largest rectangle, the shield is in the smallest rectangle (the square), and the other figure is in the second largest rectangle.
4. B. The bottom horizontal line of the first figure disappears and the bottom right vertical line in the second figure is added.

5. C. In all the others, the pattern on the outside is repeated in the center.

6. D. Matching triangles in the same position of the first three hexagons cancel each other out. If all three triangles match, then the position in the fourth hexagon is a blank.

7. B. Each of the three shapes, even though they are of different sizes, appears black, white, and striped.

8. B. At each stage the top left-hand line is moving through half the length of one side clockwise.

9. C. E and G are a mirror image, as are A and F, and B and D.

10. A. The center geometric shape adds on an additional side. All dots change from white to black, and vice versa.

11. B. The large half-circle moves from right to top to left to bottom. The medium half-circle alternates from left to right. The small half-circle moves from bottom to right to top to left. The center dot alternates between appearing and disappearing.

12. E. A is the same as G. F is the same as B. C is the same as D.

13. D. When two figures touch, they disappear at the next stage and are replaced by two different figures.

14. 20. 4 + 3 + 6 + 5 + 2 = 20. The opposite sides of a die always add to 7.

15. $6\frac{3}{7}$ square units

Visual Test 2

1. E. The diamond rotates 90°. The square goes inside the diamond. The semi-circle rotates 180° and moves to the top.

2. B. There are two alternate sequences in which a larger circle is added at each stage.

3. B. A is the same as D. C is the same as E.

4. D. The dot in the top left-hand quarter moves backward and forward between two corners, as does the dot in the bottom left-hand quarter.

The dot in the top right-hand quarter moves one corner counterclockwise at each stage and the dot in the bottom right-hand quarter moves one corner clockwise.

5. F. This way, each row and column contains four white stars and five black stars.

6. D. Working counterclockwise, the large circle is losing one quarter of its circumference at each stage. The small circle is increasing by a quarter of its circumference at each counterclockwise stage.

7. E. It contains a circle in a triangle, a black dot in a diamond, a white circle in a black circle, and a black triangle in a circle.

8. E. All the others consist of three identical figures when rotated. E has only two figures which when rotated are identical.

9. A

10. B. The symbols change position as in the example.

11. E. A is the same as B rotated. C is the same as G rotated. D is the same as F rotated.

12. A. R + S = T; X + Y = Z. But similar symbols disappear.

13. E

14. E. All the others have a matching circle rotated 90° (B-G, C-D, E-F).

15. 318°.

A. $\dfrac{360°}{4} = 90°$ 90°

B. $\dfrac{360°}{5} = 72°$ $180° - 72° = 108°$

C. $\dfrac{360°}{6} = 60°$ $180° - 60° = 120°$

$90° + 108° + 120° = 318°$

Visual Test 3

1. C. In all the others, the black circle is directly connected to three white circles.

2. C. The bottom right-hand quarter increases in size and becomes the main figure. The two components that previously made up the main figure go inside the new main figure.

3. 17

4. H. In all the others, the figure on the outside is repeated in the middle.

5. A. The third pentagon of each row and column contains only lines that appear twice in the same position in the first two pentagons. However, these lines change from straight to curved and vice versa.

6. H. All the others have a mirror-image pairing.

7. D. Then the dot appears in the diamond and one circle.

8. C

9. D. A is the same as F. B is the same as E. C is the same as G.

10. A

11. C

12. D

13. 2A

14. +. The order of the symbols is:
x + o x ≈ □

15. B

Numerical Test 1

1. 41: $7 \times 8 - 15 = 41$

2. 4763. Reverse the previous number and add 1 to the same digit each time.

3. 8. In opposite segments, alternate pairs of digits total the same.
19 + 3 = 14 + 8

4. 9598: 5217 + 4381 = 9598

5. 1: 3 × 8 – 6 = 18
Similarly: 6 × 9 – 5 = 49

6. 3824   116   17
4968   144   18
7519   130   13
32 + 84 = 116, 16 + 1 = 17

7. 12. All the other numbers are a quarter of, or four times, another number: 18/72, 5/20, 9/36, 4/16.

8. 2½ kg.

9. 22
$(7 \times 8) - (5 \times 4) = 36$
$(9 \times 3) - (5 \times 2) = 17$
$(8 \times 5) - (6 \times 3) = 22$

10. $\dfrac{166}{999}$

$$1000x = 166.166166\ldots$$
$$1x = .166166\ldots$$
$$999x = 166$$
$$x = \frac{166}{999}$$

11. 10. Each side adds up to 50.

12. 42: $(5 \times 8) - 7 = 33$
        $(6 \times 7) - 6 = 36$

$$(7 \times 5) - 4 = 31$$
$$(8 \times 7) - 14 = 42$$

13. 8. Add the top row of numbers to the second row to obtain the bottom row; i.e., 42986 + 38795 = 81781

14. 15. Add 1, 2, 3, and repeat.

15. 68: $(8 \times 9) - 3 = 69$
$$(7 \times 5) - 6 = 29$$
$$(4 \times 7) - 9 = 19$$
$$(9 \times 8) - 4 = 68$$

Numerical Test 2

1. 28

2. 7

3. 9: $39^2 = 1521$
Similarly: $76^2 = 5776$

4. 12. The outer number added to its two connected numbers always totals 20. For example: 3 + 7 + 10 = 20, 7 + 4 + 9 = 20, etc.

5. 16: 7 + 2 − 2 + 9 = 16

6. 2. Each row and column alternate sums of 19 and 17.

7. 216. The number in the center of each figure is the cube of the number of sides of the figure.

8. 27. The total of three numbers is 72 (24 x 3). The total of two numbers is 45 (22½ x 2). The third number must be 27 (72 − 45).

9. 60: 60 + 9(15%) = 69

10. 40. There are 2 series:

(+ 3¼) 27, 30¼, 33½, 36¾, 40

(−3¼) 27, 23¾, 20½, 17¼, 14

11. 4: $(39 - 3) \div 4 = 9$

$(54 - 6) \div 8 = 6$

$(45 - 36) \div 9 = 1$

$(35 - 7) \div 7 = 4$

12. 92: $12 + 6 + 7 = 25$; Reverse = 52

$17 + 9 + 9 = 35$; Reverse = 53

$7 + 4 + 8 = 19$; Reverse = 91

$11 + 13 + 5 = 29$; Reverse = 92

13. 41. The first column has even numbers starting at 26. The second column has odd numbers starting at 27. The third column has prime numbers starting at 29. The fourth column has square numbers starting at 25.

14. D. It is a perfect cube (3^3). The rest are all perfect squares.

15. 30:

$$\frac{7 \times 4 \times 3}{6} = 14$$

$$\frac{9 \times 2 \times 6}{6} = 18$$

$$\frac{12 \times 2 \times 4}{6} = 16$$

$$\frac{9 \times 4 \times 5}{6} = 30$$

Numerical Test 3

1. 25746. Multiply the previous number by 8 and add 2 each time.

2. 31. Start at 1 and work clockwise to each segment, adding 3, 6, 9, 12, 15, 18.

3. 9. Look across to same sections in each of the three figures: 4, 6, 8 (increase by 2); 9, 7, 5 (reduce by 2); 8, 5, 2 (reduce by 3); 1, 5, 9 (increase by 4).

4. 9. Looking across, rows having two numbers total 14, rows having three numbers total 18, and rows having four numbers total 22.

5. 210: $7 \times 6 \times 1 \times 5 = 210$

6. 11: $\dfrac{19 + 25}{4} = 11$

7. 5827 in the top and 1826 in the bottom. Each of the other numbers has anagram pairings top and bottom: 4829/2894, 7136/6731, 6483/8346, 9514/1459, 6127/7621, 3816/6813.

8. 18: $16 \times 9 = 8x$

$144 = 8x$

$18 = x$

9. 173: $87 + 86 = 173$

10. 46. Beginning at 17, go across the row and then follow the direction of the arrows alternating between +9 and –5.

11. LQ

12. 19

	7	12	9
+6	13	18	15
–2	11	16	13
+6	17	22	19

13. 2. Subtract the sum of the even numbers from the sum of the odd numbers.

$7 + 9 = 16$ $9 + 3 = 12$

$2 + 4 = 6$ $4 + 6 = 10$

$16 - 6 = 10$ $12 - 10 = 2$

14. 11: $(42 \div 7) + 6 = 12$
$(91 \div 13) + 4 = 11$
$(88 \div 11) + 5 = 13$
$(27 \div 9) + 8 = 11$

15. 49. Add the sum of the two digits in each box to the number to get the number in the next box. For example, $1 + 6 = 7; 7 + 16 = 23$.

Numerical Test 4

1. 212: $7 \times 3 = 21, 1 + 1 = 2$

2. 9. Looking across each row of numbers, the bottom row totals 5, the fourth row totals 6, the third row totals 7, and the second row totals 8. Therefore, the top row should total 9.

3. 41. These are the prime numbers from 17 to 41.

4. 32. Multiply by 3 and add 2 to obtain the pairings:
$10 \times 3 = 30; 30 + 2 = 32$

The other such pairs are: 3/11, 7/23, 20/62, 2/8, 16/50, and 15/47.

5. 9: $16 \times 6 = 96$; Similarly: $29 \times 3 = 87$ and $15 \times 5 = 75$

6.
A	B	C	D	E
2	4	3	7	11
10	5	13	9	7
22	23	17	19	18
36	39	40	41	40

$A + C = B$ in the row below.
$C + D = A$ in the row below.
$A + E = C$ in the row below.
$B + C = E$ in the row below.
$A + D = D$ in the row below.

7. $\frac{1}{6}$

8. $802/1125.1000x = 712.888888...$

$$x = \quad .712888...$$
$$999x = 712.176$$
$$999000x = 712176$$
$$x = \frac{712176}{999000}$$
$$x = \frac{802}{1125}$$

9. 99. There are 2 series: $(+4\frac{1}{4})$ 82, $86\frac{1}{4}$, $90\frac{1}{2}$, $94\frac{3}{4}$, 99

$\qquad\qquad\qquad\qquad\qquad (-4\frac{1}{4})$ 82, $77\frac{3}{4}$, $73\frac{1}{2}$, $69\frac{1}{4}$

10. 4

11. 135°: $\dfrac{360°}{8} = 45°$

$\qquad\quad 180° - 45° = 135°$

12. 28: $(6 + 7) \times 4 = 52$

$\qquad\quad (8 + 5) \times 3 = 39$

$\qquad\quad (4 + 3) \times 8 = 56$

$\qquad\quad (5 + 2) \times 4 = 28$

13. 10879. Add the number to the reverse of its digits.
For example: $163 + 361 = 524$, etc.

14. 14: LH $\qquad\qquad$ RH

$\qquad\quad 5 \times 14 = 70 \qquad 3 \times 9 = 27$

$\qquad\quad 1 \times 10 = 10 \qquad 6 \times 8 = 48$

$\qquad\qquad\qquad\qquad\quad 1 \times 5 = \underline{\;\;5\;\;}$

$\qquad\qquad\quad \overline{\quad 80 \quad} \qquad\qquad \overline{\quad 80 \quad}$

15. LM

Numerical Test 5

1. 110: The sequence progresses -1×2, -2×2, -3×2, -4×2, -5×2
So: $60 - 5 = 55$; $55 \times 2 = 110$

2. 19: $3 \times 9 = 27$; $27 - 8 = 19$

3. 8429. In all the others, the last two digits multiplied together is equal to the first two digits.

4. 1716: 39×44

5. 3: $6 \times 7 = 42$, $7 \times 2 = 14$; $42 \div 14 = 3$

6. 16. There are two alternate sequences that increase by 2 and 5, respectively, i.e., 1, 3, 5, 7 and 1, 6, 11, 16.

7. 32: $4 - 1 = 3$ and $9 - 7 = 2$

8. 130: $+18$, $+20$, $+22$, $+24$

9. 132: $7 + 1^3 = 8$
$7 + 2^3 = 15$
$7 + 3^3 = 34$
$7 + 4^3 = 71$
$7 + 5^3 = 132$

10. 171:

1st CIRCLE	2nd CIRCLE	3rd CIRCLE
$17 \times 4 = 68$	$7 \times 6 = 42$	$21 \times 9 = 189$
$13 \times 4 = 52$	$11 \times 6 = 66$	$14 \times 9 = 126$
$19 \times 4 = 76$	$16 \times 6 = 96$	$19 \times 9 = 171$

11. 12:

$10 + 11 + 13 + 5 = 39$; $39 \div 3 = 13$
$17 + 5 + 9 + 17 = 48$; $48 \div 3 = 16$
$19 + 6 + 7 + 10 = 42$; $42 \div 3 = 14$
$9 + 15 + 6 + 6 = 36$; $36 \div 3 = 12$

12. 4: $4^2 + 3^2 = 25$

$\quad\quad\quad 6^2 + 2^2 = 40$

$\quad\quad\quad 7^2 + 5^2 = 74$

$\quad\quad\quad 5^2 + 4^2 = 41$

13. 831. The number sequence 1724683 repeats.

14. 1:

$$\frac{17}{19} \div \frac{68}{38} \div \frac{16}{32} = \frac{17}{19} \times \frac{38}{68} \times \frac{32}{16} = 1$$

15.

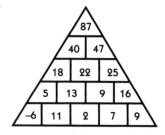

Calculation and Logic Test 1

1. G

2. 37 minutes

3. Jim 28, Alf 42, Sid 63. 28 + 14 = 42, 42 + 21 = 63

4. TRUCULENT. Each word starts with the letter in the alphabet following the last letter of the previous word. The length of the words increases by one each time.

5. Lemon = 60¢, orange = 80¢

6. 11 PM

7. 29 apples into 23 bags. 667 is the product of two prime numbers, 23 and 29. The smaller of these two numbers is the number of bags, as you wish to use the smallest number of bags possible.

8. ⅘

9. $C = \dfrac{9}{5} F + 32$

$F = \dfrac{5}{9} (C - 32)$

10. 80: $\dfrac{60 \times 20}{15} = 80$

16 slices = 15 cuts

11. 25 ft x 25 ft. 15 ft x 15 ft.

12. 107: $99 - (4 \times 9) = 63$

$63 + (4 \times 11) = 107$

13. C. It has five right angles. The others have four right angles.

14. 210 days. $5 \times 6 \times 7$

15. Find the center point S/N + E/W of the six dots. The answer is C4.

Calculation and Logic Test 2

1. Bill.

2. B. They are the letters K, L, M, and N on their side. So O is the next one.

3. BRIEF.

1 3   2 (1 2 3 4 5) 5   4

B I K E R (B R I E F) R I F L E

4. 1 minute 12 seconds:

$\dfrac{(1.25 + 0.25) \times 60}{75} = \dfrac{1.5 \times 60}{75}$ = 1.2 minutes or 1 minute 12 seconds

5. 168 lbs. 75% × 168 = 126; 126 + 42 = 168

6. Originally, Frasier had sixteen, Niles had eight, and Daphne had four. Then Daphne lost one, which meant she had three. She gave two to Frasier and one to Niles. This meant Frasier had eighteen and Niles had nine.

7. 10:00. The big hand moves two back at each stage and the small hand moves three forward.

8. Say that the kennel costs $k and the dog $d.

Then

$k = \dfrac{1}{3}(k + d + 5)$

$d = \dfrac{3}{4}(d + k - 5)$

Then

$2k - d = 5$ and

$3k - d = 15$

So $k = 10$ and $d = 15$.

The dog costs $15 and the kennel costs $10.

9. 441 sq. ft. and 49 sq. ft.

10. One person had a piece on a plate.

11. 2147

2147

+418

─────

4712

12. 54 years

13. Alice is 16, Barbara is 60, and Chloe is 80.

14. 4¾ kg.

$$\text{LH} \qquad\qquad \text{RH}$$

$$4 \text{ kg} \times 4 = 16 \quad 6 \text{ kg} \times 2 = 12$$

$$5 \text{ kg} \times 3 = \underline{15} \quad 4¾ \times 4 = \underline{19}$$

$$\qquad\qquad 31 \qquad\qquad\quad 31$$

15. $15 \ (2^4 - 1)$

Calculation and Logic Test 3

1. 21

2. 4 minutes

$$\frac{1}{4.5} + \frac{1}{12} - \frac{1}{18} = .25$$

$$\frac{1}{.25} = 4$$

3. Five; one of each in brown, blue, gray, green, and black.

4. The second option.

First option ($2000 increase after 12 months)

First year: $20,000 + $20,000 = $40,000

Second year: $21,000 + $21,000 = $42,000

Second option ($500 increase after 6 months)

First year: $20,000 + $20,500 = $40,500

Second year: $21,000 + $21,500 = $42,500

5. King of Hearts

6. Seventy-three people paid $39.

7. There are 13 lions and 17 eagles.

8. WEDNESDAY

9. 64. Question 1: No. 42 to 82.

Question 2: Yes. 44 – 48 – 52 – 56 – 60 – 68 – 72 – 76 – 80.

Question 3: Yes. 64.

10. They were playing pool in the club house.

11. 729. Statement 1 is a lie. The only square and cube number between 99 and 999 whose first and last digits are 5, 7, or 9 is 729.

12. 2519

13. Arthur would take 60 days. Bert would take 40 days.

14. 4027
      × 2
    ――――
     8054

15. $3456

Calculation and Logic Test 4

1.

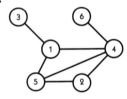

2. 39 socks. If he takes out 37 socks, although it's a long shot, they could be all blue and red. To be 100% certain that he has a pair of gray socks, he must take out two more.

3. 37.5 minutes

$$\frac{50 \times 24}{32}$$

4. 1243. Reverse the digits and drop the largest number each time.

5. 2050

6. Newspaper $1.80, magazine $3.00

7. TOGETHER: pl**A**ce**B**os

se**C**lu**D**ed

sp**E**ci**F**ic

to**G**et**H**er

8. 29. A vowel = 3, a consonant = 5.

9. The land doesn't exist. For a triangle to exist, the two smaller sides must be longer than the third side. It is an impossible triangle.

10. True. There must be one or the other.

11. 32. Say this is x, then, 3 ($\frac{1}{2}$x + 1) + 4 = x + 23

x = 32

12. $22,781.25

13. 8111$\frac{1}{2}$

14. Tony is 7 years old. Margaret is 13 years old.

15.

Guilty	Truth spoken by
Jack	Alan, Sid, and George
George	Jack and Sid
Alan	Sid and George
Sid	George alone

So SID was the culprit.

Calculation and Logic Test 5

1. D

2. $6500

3. Tom is 32, Dick is 40, and Harry is 50.

ANSWERS
Warm Ups

4. E. 42198

A	B	C	D	E
9	1	4	8	2
C	E	B	A	D
4	2	1	9	8

5. One chance in 210.

6. Tom has 42, Dick has 28, and Harry has 14.

7. No calculations are necessary. Obviously they will be both the same distance from Dallas when they meet, and they will both be the same distance from Detroit!

8. The number on the left is in base 9, and the number on the right is in base 10.

$41 \rightarrow 37$

9. 56: $8 \times 7 = 56$

10. 204:

$1^2, 2^2, 3^2, 4^2, 5^2, 6^2, 7^2, 8^2$

$1 + 4 + 9 + 16 + 25 + 36 + 49 + 64$

11. 4⅔ lb. ⅔ of a pound plus 5/7 of its weight = complete weight. Hence, ⅔ of a pound equals 1/7 of its weight. So it weighs 7 x ⅔ lb.

12. 36 (6^2). The first column are odd numbers, the second column are even numbers, the third are prime numbers, and the fourth are square numbers.

13. A had $2.50. B had $4.

14. 125. If you add 125 to 100 and to 164, you get two square numbers, 225 and 289, the squares of 15 and 17.

15. Say the first digit of her age is x.

Then her age in years is 10x + 3; its reverse is 30 + x.

Then: $x^2 = 30 + x$; Hence x = 6

Her age is 63 years.

IQ TESTERS

Test 1

1. Floor (changing the d in flood)

2. The letters increase by 3, and the numbers decrease by 8.

W
37

3. Friday.

The pairs below show: (day, number of toys after donation)

(Sun, 31), (Mon, 15), (Tue, 7), (Wed, 3), (Thu 1), (Fri, 0).

4. DIVIDE AND CONQUER

5. 8 o'clock.

If the clock just finished striking, it has struck three consecutive hours in the last 2½ hours: the one it just struck, the one it struck an hour ago, and the one it struck two hours ago.

The sum: 6 + 7 + 8 = 21

6. A

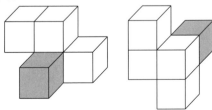

7. Add seven C's to form these bones:

CLAVICLE, SCAPULA, SACRUM, COCCYX

8. REBEL PEBBLE

9. BEGINNER'S LUCK

10. 14.

Add the numbers outside each triangle to make the number within.

The calculation: $4 + 4 + 6 = 14$

11. N4.

These are the initial letters of each number from one to nine followed by the number of letters its word contains. Since the word NINE starts with N and has four letters in it, the next term is N4.

12. 11.

If the number were divisible by any other two-digit palindrome, then it would also be divisible by 11. So the answer must be 11 only.

13. ELEPHANT, ARMADILLO, ANTELOPE

14. SCARLET, CARMINE, CRIMSON.

All of these are shades of red.

15. LILIES & LILACS.

Insert the letters L, I, L, S.

Test 2

1. SKIN & BONES

2. N.

The three words formed are RANGE, SNACK, and ARENA.

3. June 9.

Although Gillian gains 3 treats per day, the date on which she first has 60 treats in the house is the day after she was left with 54 treats, because her morning purchase raises the number of treats in the house to 60. She had 30 treats left on the evening of May 31. In 8 days, gaining 3 treats per day, she has 54 treats in the evening. The next morning, June 9, she buys 6 more to bring the total to 60 for the first time.

4. CF, AH, EG, DB

hook (C), line (F), and sinker

lock (A), stock (H), and barrel

bacon (E), lettuce (G), and tomato

rock (D), paper (B), and scissors

5. Truffle

6. 30.

Add up the values for each letter in the word.

POODLE = 9 + 10 + 10 + 3 + 6 + 8 = 46

DALMATIAN = 3 + 1 + 6 + 4 + 1 + 5 + 2 + 1 + 7 = 30

(Make sure you spell "Dalmatian" correctly!)

7. IV.

The entire pattern is a palindrome.

8.

A	B	C
5	3	4
D	E	F
1	9	2

If each row across totals 12, then the sum of all six numbers is 24. Since the middle column is half the sum of all six numbers, it totals 12. Since E = 9, we know that B = 3. In the bottom row, the sum is 12, and since E = 9, the values of D and F must be 1 and 2 in some order. The outside columns add up to 6, so A and C are the numbers 5 and 4. But A must be the largest number in its row, so A = 5, C = 4, D = 1, and F = 2.

9. SOWS, SONS, SINS, SINK, OINK

10. TRAGIC

11. $1\frac{1}{2}$

We need $3x = x + 3$, so $2x = 3$, or $x = \frac{3}{2}$ (or $1\frac{1}{2}$).

12. 8 and 4.

Subtract 7, divide by 2, subtract 7, divide by 2, and so on.

Thus, the calculation is $15 - 7 = 8$, and then $8 \div 2 = 4$.

13. Saxophone

14. APPROACH & UMBRELLA

15. CHOP

(c)limber, (h)eight, (o)range, (p)lumber

Test 3

1. STONE.

The replacement letter is S. The words formed are cheSt, laSer, Spine, cloSe, purSe. The circled letters spell atone, which can be changed to Stone.

2. 19 blocks. There are four layers. From the top down, they could have at maximum 1 block, 4 blocks, 9 blocks, and 5 blocks.

3. ENTRENCH, POSTPONE, TOMATOES, CETACEAN

4. 96.

Method 1: Fran's total points collected on the first three tests are $3 \times 76 = 228$. But Fran wants to have a total of $4 \times 81 = 324$ for the four tests. She needs to score $324 - 228 = 96$.

Method 2: On each of the first three tests, Fran is short $81 - 76 = 5$ points of her goal. On the last test she must compensate for these and score $81 + (3 \times 5) = 96$.

5. YEAST.

These are all anagrams of SEAT with one extra letter added. The letters added, in order, are R, S, T, U, V, W, X, Y.

6. cHATEau & gLOVE

7. BCDA

Words that rhyme:

fender/blender, carrot/parrot, poodles/noodles, stencil/pencil

8. GELATIN.

Move the G from the end to the beginning.

9. C.

Move back 1, then 2, then 3, then 4, then 5, then 6.

The letter 6 places before I is C.

10. CORNCOB has the same substitution pattern as LEAFLET.

11. PIECRUSTS, CANOEISTS, MOUNTAINEER

12. SLEIGH.

Type each number into a calculator and then turn the calculator upside down to read the words.

13. 48.

Each number is the product of the number of sides in the shape enclosing it, multiplied by its position in the sequence. Since the octagon has 8 sides and is 6th in the sequence, the number inside it should be $8 \times 6 = 48$.

14. SCREECHED

15. 181.

Add the squares of the two numbers at the top of each triangle to get the number at the bottom.
The calculation: $(9 \times 9) + (10 \times 10) = 181$

Test 4

1. PLUTO (or JULIE).

The only five-letter planets are VENUS, EARTH, and PLUTO, and by using their shared letters (E, T, and U) you can match them up in the coded sentence and decode the remainder. The question reads, "Is Venus, Pluto, or Earth farthest from the Sun?"

2. ANIMALS

HORSE, SNAKE, CAMEL, ZEBRA, RACCOON, PORCUPINE, ARMADILLO

3. GROSSER GROCER

4. Needless, needles

5. 7655.

The rule is $3 \times (\text{previous}) - 1$, so the calculation is $3 \times 2552 - 1 = 7655$.

6. AUTHOR

7. $6/2 = 9/3$

8. PUB GAME

9. 6½ square units.

One way to solve this is to divide up the grid into triangles. The area of a triangle is half its base times its height. Each of the triangles below has an area of one-half square units, and there are 13 such triangles, so the total area is $13 \times \frac{1}{2} = 6\frac{1}{2}$ square units.

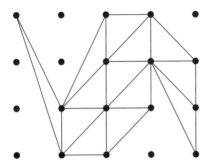

10. SKI.

The three words formed are RISKING, SKIFF, and OILSKIN.

11. L.

The three words formed are PLAIN, MULCH, and MANLY.

12. 993 times.

There are 20 fives in the tens and ones places of one hundred numbers (10 in the ones place and 10 in the tens place). In each of the 500's, 1500's, and 2500's there are 100 more fives in the hundreds places. So from 1 to 3400 there are $(34 \times 20) + (3 \times 100) = 980$ fives. And from 3400 to 3456 there are 13 more fives, for a total of $980 + 13 = 993$ fives.

13. CONGRATULATIONS.

The countries' first letters give the consonants.

For the vowels,

Vip! = A

Wip! = E (not used)

Xip! = I

Yip! = O

Zip! = U

14. Add six F's to form these animals:

WOLF, GIRAFFE, BUFFALO, FERRET

15. 12.

The two numbers in the left column have the same product as the two numbers in the right column. The calculation: $8 \times 9 \div 6 = 12$

Test 5

1. 1881

2. A.

The pictures represent a sequence of four-letter words that overlap by two letters. The sequence is Lima, mane, nest, star, arch, chin.

3. Maroon, desert, strand

4. SINGLE TINGLE

5. A. deck.

The lowercase word is a definition for a word hidden in the upper-case word. The hidden words are LEVEL, TROPHY, FELINE, CHIMED, and PATIO.

6. VIOLET & PURPLE
BUTTER & SIZZLE
SUMMER & WINTER

7. IF YOU CAN FIGURE THIS OUT YOU CAN IGNORE VOWELS!
All of the vowels are replaced by 3's.

8. HATE, HAVE, CAVE, COVE, LOVE
HATE, HAVE, RAVE, ROVE, LOVE

9. TH & TH.
This sequence consists of the last pair of letters in the words fir<u>st</u>, seco<u>nd</u>, thi<u>rd</u>, four<u>th</u>, fif<u>th</u>, six<u>th</u>.

10. WRITHE

11. Delicious, delirious

12. LEMON.
The words formed are: OWLS, CHEW, TIME, ATOP, and LENT.

13. F720.
The letters move back and forth by powers of two:
−1 +2 −4 +8 −16.
The numbers multiply each time by a number one higher:
×2 ×3 ×4 ×5 ×6.
The letter 16 places before V is F.
The number is calculated 120 × 6 = 720.

14. E D A C B
E. Blusher = red one
D. Show pain = yell "ow!"
A. Personal automobile = car mine
C. Jokester = pun gent
B. Demonstrator = show-er

15. TOUGH & SCUFF
STEIN & WHINE
PASTE & WAIST

Test 6

1.

W	A	F	T	S
A	L	E	R	T
R	O	T	O	R
T	H	E	T	A
S	A	S	S	Y

2. P.

The three words formed are RAPID, SPEAR, and COOPT.

3. CRYPTIC.

The words, when read aloud, spell CRYPTIC.

4. 97.

Add three more each time: +1 +4 +7 +10 +13 +16 +19 +22

The calculation: 75 + 22 = 97

5. A. SIT, FIST, STIFF

  B. HITS, SHIFT, FIFTHS

  C. HIRES, FISHER, SHERIFF

6. COLUMNIST

mocCasin	C
violOncello	O
pavilion	L
guttUral	U
accomModate	M
inoculate	N
idIosyncrasy	I
conSensus	S
diletTante	T

7. LOOK BEFORE YOU LEAP

8. Transom

9. cLOSEt & tWINge

10. AIR BED, inflated

  JET SET, affluent

  OLD HAT, outdated

  HOT ROD, mechanic

  POTPIE, victuals

11. All three.

Bob's mother always works. If Bob marries his father's sister's husband's sister, then Bob's wife works. If Bob's daughter marries Bob's father's sister's husband's sister, then Bob's daughter works.

12.

A	B	C
6	2	5
D	E	F
4	3	1

If A + C + E = 14, then A, C, E must be 6, 5, 3 in some order.

If B = 1 then $(1 \times 1) + 1 = 2$, and A cannot be 2. So B = 2 and A = $(2 \times 2) + 2 = 6$. The numbers C, D, E, F are 5, 4, 3, 1.

13. DCAB

Each word pictured drops its labeled letter to make a new word: ch(a)in, lim(b)o, dun(c)e, bri(d)e

14. 168°.

Since there are 360° in a circle and 60 minutes in an hour, the minute hand moves 6° per minute. From 9:34 A.M. to 10:02 A.M. is 28 minutes, so the minute hand turns $28 \times 6° = 168°$.

15. RAY

LAVA

CANAL

PAPAYA

CARAVAN

Test 7

1. Y and S.

There are two sequences interwoven.

One is the initial letters of the days of the week: S M T W T F S.

The other increases by four each time: E I M Q U Y.

2. 16.

(Smokestack – left wheel) × right wheel = body

The calculation: $(15 - 7) \times 2 = 16$

3. DAUGHTER, NIECE, BROTHER

4. 5:05

5. 46.

These are the perfect squares 9, 16, 25, 36, 49, 64, 81 written backward.

6.

R	E	H	A	B
E	X	I	L	E
A	P	P	L	E
D	E	P	O	T
S	L	O	W	S

7. MASTERFUL.

Since RAMS = 6213, FLUTE = 79845, and FARM = 7261, you can figure out our number-letter matching scheme and write the letters in numerical order. The word spelled is MASTERFUL, which describes your code-breaking ability if you got that answer.

8. The leftover letters spell COUNT.

9. Would, wood

10. O.

The three words formed are BORED, BORON, and FLOAT.

11. Add eight I's to form these periodic table elements:
IRON, IODINE, IRIDIUM, LITHIUM

12. ROOFER

13. 30 cents.

Remove $2.00 from $2.60 and the remaining $0.60 must be split between the eraser and the pencil. So the eraser costs $2.30 and the pencil costs $0.30.

14. CONDOR

FALCON

ORIOLE

TOUCAN

CUCKOO

MAGPIE

PIGEON

TURKEY

15. CLEANSE, EXPANSE

Test 8

1.

This answer grid can also be flipped along the main diagonal so that GARGLE is the first word across.

2. $12^2 = 144$

3. FLINT.

The replacement letter is L. The words formed are aLter, repLy, daLly, graiL, sLing. The circled letters spell faint, which can be changed to fLint.

4. ENEMY.

All are anagrams of world capitals except ENEMY, which is the anagram of a country, YEMEN. The other words rearrange to OSLO, PARIS, SEOUL, MANILA, QUITO.

5. 14 times

6. $8 + 8 + 8$ and $22 + 2$

7. The bonus word is REBUILT.

E	U	Q	S	I	B	S
B	Q	M	U	L	T	P
I	U	S	A	I	R	A
R	E	B	U	I	L	T
C	N	Q	B	L	Z	T
S	C	R	O	L	L	E
A	H	W	A	T	E	R

8. 6 people sit next to females.

7 people sit next to males.

9. Q.

The letter just left of the letter two below G is P.

The letter just below the letter to the right of B is H.

The letter exactly between P and H is L.

The letter directly below L is Q.

10. CADB

The words pictured are anagrams of each other:

petal/plate, beard/bread, skate/steak, earth/heart

11. Against.

I was against getting rid of the proposal.

So Joe wanted to get rid of the proposal.

12. 112 lockers.

If the lockers are numbered from 678 to 789, then the 677 lockers numbered 1 to 677 are missing from a total of 789 lockers. The number remaining is 789 − 677 = 112 lockers.

13. D (or Z).

Here's the translation:

CHOOSE THE CORRECT ANSWER:

A. DON'T TAKE ME

B. I'M PROBABLY NOT IT

C. SELECT D INSTEAD

D. WINNER'S PICK

14. CLUE.

The four-letter words appear in the odd-numbered positions in the seven-letter words.

15. S1.

Put in numerical order, the letters spell SCRAMBLED.

Test 9

1.

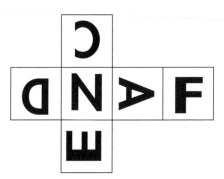

2. OPPONENT has the same substitution pattern as FOOFARAW.

3. LADY, LADS, LASS, MASS, MISS

4.

C	B		A
	A	C	B
B	C	A	
A		B	C

5. FALSEtto and misconsTRUE

6. $150.

The calculation: $165 ÷ 1.1

7.

The cards alternate hearts, spades, hearts, spades.
The values follow the pattern +2, +1, +2, +1 ...

8. ASTRONOMERS

9. The picture is an arrow.

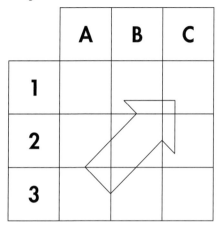

10. EMBRYO

11. 42 years old.

Method 1: If 6 people have an average age of 32 then the sum of their ages is $(6 \times 32) = 192$. If 5 people have an average age of 30 then the sum of their ages is $(5 \times 30) = 150$. The difference $192 - 150 = 42$ is the age of the sixth person.

Method 2: If the sixth person were 30, the average would stay at 30. For the average to raise to 32, each of the six people must receive on average 2 more years. Since these extra years all belong to the sixth person, the sixth person's age is $30 + (6 \times 2) = 42$.

12. FORMER, ERRATA, TAUNTS, TSETSE, SERAPH, PHYSIO, IODINE, NEBULA, LATTER

13. FOR THE RECORD.

Simply put the three words together and respace them.

14. FOOD & DRINK

15. President, resident

Test 10

1. PRAISE

2. 4, 71, E.

There are three interwoven sequences here:

128, 64, 32, 16, 8, 4 (keep dividing by 2)

61, 63, 65, 67, 69, 71 (keep adding 2)

Y, S, N, J, G, E (move 6 letters, then 5, then 4, 3, 2).

3. By matching the chess pieces up with the correct letters, you can make four words: bROOK, sinKING, sPAWN, weeKNIGHT

4. 450 inches.

There are 18 edges along the outside and each one is 25 inches. Every four edges make 100 inches, so 18 edges make 450 inches.

5. POKER becomes JOKER

6. 1.

If you add the top two numbers, you should get the same amount as dividing the bottom two numbers.

The calculation: $(20 \div 5) - 3 = 1$

7. CANDLE VANDAL

8. 5 chocolate chunks.

Making one ratio, 6 chocolate chunks = 60 jellybeans = 24 licorice sticks. So 1 chocolate chunk will balance 4 licorice sticks, which means 5 chocolate chunks will balance 20 licorice sticks.

9. CIGAR.

The last five letters of the first word are reversed to make the second word.

10. Medical

11.

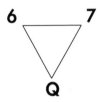

The numbers at the top left corners decrease by 17, then 15, then 13, etc.

The numbers at the top right corners are consecutive primes, descending.

The letters move up by two each time.

12. U.

The words formed are GAUZE, OUNCE, and PROUD.

13. TATTLE = 66.

If TILT = 77, the letters can only represent 1, 1, 7, 11, so T must be 1.

If TALL = 363 and T = 1, then ALL = 363. The factors of 363 are 3, 11, 11, so A = 3 and L = 11. If TEEN = 52, the factors of 52 are 2, 2, 13, so E = 2 and N = 13. We can now calculate:
TATTLE = $1 \times 3 \times 1 \times 1 \times 11 \times 2$ = 66.

14. Add six O's to make these gems:

TOPAZ, MOONSTONE, OPAL, ONYX

15. 25134.

 The digits represent the vowels in the words: A = 1, E = 2, I = 3, O = 4, U = 5.

Test 11

1. OBJECTS IN MIRROR ARE CLOSER THAN THEY APPEAR

2. 60 mph.

 Tom drove for 20 minutes (⅓ of an hour) at 90 mph, so he went 30 miles.

 Since Janice drove the same 30 miles in 30 minutes (½ of an hour), her rate was 60 mph.

3. BDAC

 Each pair of words makes a phrase or compound word:

 shoehorn, starfish, drumstick, plate glass

4. AUSTRIA, ESTONIA, ANGOLA

5.

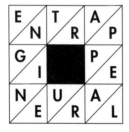

 This answer grid can also be flipped along the main diagonal so that ENGINE is the first word across.

6. 215.

Each term is the sum of the previous two.

The calculation: $82 + 133 = 215$

7. MONEY TALKS

8. WISCONSIN is the "state."

Change each of the elements listed into its one-letter periodic table abbreviation.

9. TRAWL.

The replacement letter is W. The words formed are alloW, Wound, Wired, draWn, sWing. The circled letters spell trail, which can be changed to traWl.

10. 10 marbles.

If Paul has p marbles, then

$5p + p + 5 + p = 75$. So $7p = 70$ and $p = 10$.

11. OUTLAY.

If S = shaded and U = unshaded, the landings are:

A	B	C
S	U	O
U	S	U
S	S	T
S	U	L
S	U	A
U	S	Y

12. CHINTZ

13. 91 cubes.

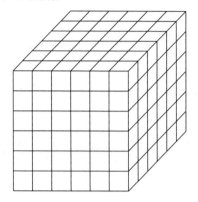

Method 1: You can see three faces at once. You can see one face only of 25 blocks on each of the three faces, for a total of 75 blocks. You can see two faces of 5 blocks along each of the three edges visible, for a total of 15 blocks. Finally, you can see three sides of the one corner block that is facing you. The total number of blocks you can see is 75 + 15 + 1 = 91.

Method 2: If you remove all of the blocks you can see, you are left with a 5 × 5 × 5 cube that you cannot see. There are 6 × 6 × 6 = 216 blocks in all and you cannot see 5 × 5 × 5 = 125 of them. So you can see 216 − 125 = 91 blocks.

14. QUIET & QUITE

ALOFT & FLOAT

BUGLE & BULGE

15. NUCLEI

Test 12

1. CDBA

   Two meanings of each word are pictured:

   bowler, runner, pitcher, boxers

2. CHOWDER POWDER

3. IF YOU MUST DO IT, DO IT WELL.

   The words are: TIFF, JOYOUS, MUSTARD, ENDOW, DITCH, ADOPT, SUITE, DWELLING.

4. 37 palindromes.

   The three-digit patterns from 700 to 999 are 7d7, 8d8, and 9d9, where d can be replaced by any of the 10 digits from 0 to 9. This makes 30 palindromes. The four-digit patterns are 1dd1, where d can be any of the digits 0, 1, 2, 3, 4, 5, 6. This makes 7 more palindromes. The total is 30 + 7 = 37 palindromes.

5. BDAC.

   Although the words look like they're in English, each is the French word for its respective picture. The French bread provides a clue.

6. On the 7th turn.

   The numbers in this diagram show the square landed on on each turn:

2			3	6
1,5				
7				4

7. COMEdy & biGOt

8. Condone, condo

9. 31

Keep subtracting the next even number: –4 –6 –8 –10 –12 –14 –16.

The calculation: 47 – 16 = 31

10. FRET SAW

11. CADRE.

Each shorter word is a synonym of the longer word that is found in its correct order from left to right in the longer word.

12. $80.

The total cost is $240, so each person should pay $120.

13. BROAH.

The anagrams are: ADORE, CHERISH, ENJOY, ABHOR, IDOLIZE.

14. 90 is the total.

You don't actually need to find the values of the symbols. Just add up the across totals (155 + 120 + 115 + 115 = 505) and subtract the sum of the three down totals given (145 + 110 + 160 = 415). The difference (505 – 415 = 90) must be the total of the last column. For the record, though:

▲ = 15   ■ = 30

● = 25   ◆ = 50

15. R.

The words formed are ERASE, LEARN, and MORON.

Test 13

1. Thursday.

The division $4400 \div 7$ gives 628 remainder 4. This means that 628 weeks go by and there are 4 extra days. This puts us at Thursday.

2. Y.

These are the words EMPTY and FULL interspersed.

3. 30 games.

It takes $4 + 3 + 2 + 1 = 10$ games for every team to play every other team once. So it takes 30 games for every team to play every other team three times.

4. Five.

The numbers are 7, 19, 3, 17, 2. The number 15 is not prime because it is 3×5.

5. BARIUM
CARBON
COBALT
COPPER
IODINE
NICKEL
OXYGEN
SILVER
SODIUM

6. RITUAL

7. CADB.

Each word in the top row takes an apostrophe and an s and then joins with the word represented by its picture to make a common phrase. The phrases formed are: mare's nest, crow's feet, writer's block, fool's gold.

8. ARROW.

The words formed are: BASE, ORCA, ORES, ZONE, EWES.

9. 3.

Subtracting the product of the outside numbers from the middle number in the strip gives the circled number.
The calculation: $13 - (2 \times 5) = 3$

10. 243.

Each term is the previous one multiplied by $\frac{3}{2}$.

11. CAST IRON STOMACH.

CAST makes "plaster cast" and "cast anchor."
IRON makes "steam iron" and "iron maiden."
STOMACH makes "weak stomach" and "stomach flu."

12. The lemon.

The other items are all red or traditionally red.

13. GENERAL MANAGER.

The key is that 0123456 = AEGLMNR. Change the number on each half of each domino to its corresponding letter. The top halves spell GENERAL and the bottom halves spell MANAGER.

14. HASTE MAKES WASTE

15. Add seven N's to make these seasonings:
CINNAMON, CUMIN, GINGER, FENNEL

Test 14

1. Outraced

2. 7.

   The square of 7 is 49. The sum $4 + 9$ equals 13. And 13 is 6 greater than 7.

3. Squash, cricket, polo

4. 9 performances.

   We can have a performance the first day, and then every third day after that, giving 8 more performances. The total: $1 + 8 = 9$

5. UTO.

   These are the last three letters of each of the names of the planets in our solar system: MercURY, VeNUS, EaRTH, MARS, JupiTER, SatURN, UraNUS, NeptUNE, PlUTO.

6. AWE.

   The words formed are DRAWER, SEAWEED, and OUTLAWED.

7. OUT OF SIGHT, OUT OF MIND

8. FRANCE.

   The capital of Germany (Berlin) is hidden in TIM<u>BERLIN</u>E.

   The capital of France (Paris) is hidden in COM<u>PARIS</u>ON.

9. DO AS I SAY, NOT AS I DO

10. CE BH DF AG

    The words pictured in the top row get inserted into the words pictured in the bottom row to make new words or phrases.

    b(egg)ar, pi(rat)e, t(urn)ip, w(ant) ad

11. 0.3

Divide by 2, then by 3, then by 4, then by 5, then by 6.

The calculation: $1.8 \div 6 = 0.3$

12. Q and U.

R is three months after T, so T and R are in October & January or in November & February. But they can't be in October & January because then V and X cannot be in the same month. Now V & X are either in October or January. If they're in October, then there is no month in which Q is performed, so V & X are done in January. This puts P in December and Q & U in October.

13. I.

The words formed are TACIT, MOIST, and PILOT.

14. The phrase is NARROW ESCAPE.

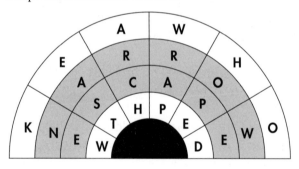

15. 17 regular employees.

Not including the president, the company collected $170 from 20 employees. If r is the number of regular employees and v is the number of vice presidents, then $r + v = 20$ and $7r + 17v = 170$. Solve by elimination or substitution to find that $r = 17$.

Test 15

1. ECABD.

   The initial letters of each phrase spell the answer.

   For example, the initial letters of "put out to sea" spell POTS.

2. PARTNER.

   Each word has its final letter removed and is written backward. The question reads: "What seven-letter word meaning 'business associate' will become another word meaning 'capture' when you remove its final letter and turn it backward?" The answer is PARTNER, which becomes ENTRAP.

3. EL.

   The words formed are: DELIVER, PRELUDE, GRAVELY, and TANGELO.

4.

This answer grid can also be flipped along the main diagonal so that GARISH is the first word across.

5. 52 houses.

Consecutive even numbers from 28 to 130 is the same as consecutive numbers from 14 to 65. The number of numbers is 65 numbers minus the 13 numbers from 1 to 13.
The calculation: $65 - 13 = 52$

6. orcHARD and quEASY

7. Three times.

The ace and five simply switch back and forth, while the 2, 6, 3, and 4 are in a rotating cycle of four. The next three presses of the button give the following orders: A32654 then 5642A3 and finally A23456.

8. FIELD & STREAM

9. STATUS

10. 10 numbers.

They are: 3, 30, 300, 12, 21, 102, 120, 201, 210, 111

11. A, B, OR C

12. BASEBALL has the same substitution pattern as NEATNESS.

13. A.

The word "sickle" is heard at the end of the word "bicycle."

The word "meringue" is heard at the end of the word "boomerang."

14. 20 and 5.

Add 2, divide by 4, add 2, divide by 4.

15. D.

Top circle moves to position 4.

Second circle stays in place.

Third circle is copied to positions 3 and 5.

Fourth circle moves to position 1.

Fifth circle does not appear.

Test 16

1. Four combinations.

   They are: (6, 5, 2), (6, 4, 3), (5, 5, 3), (5, 4, 4).

2. 7.

   Keep subtracting the next power of 3: $-1\ -3\ -9\ -27\ -81\ -243$

   The calculation: $250 - 243 = 7$

3. The phrase is MIX IT ALL UP.

S	M	E	A	R
R	I	F	L	E
E	X	A	L	T
P	I	Q	U	E
S	T	O	P	S

4. Better late than never. (Better never late!)

5. HEAVEN & TREMOR

6. H.

   The words formed are SHAME, LATHE, and USHER.

7. THE TAIL OF A MOUSE.

   Simply respace the letters given.

8. 10 combinations.

If the pins are A, B, C, D, and E, the 10 combinations are AB, AC, AD, AE, BC, BD, BE, CD, CE, DE.

9. Add seven C's to make these drinks:

COCOA, COGNAC, COFFEE, CURAÇAO

10. NORTH (or CAMEL).

You can match the compass points with the underlined words by examining lengths and shared letters in NORTH, SOUTH, EAST, and WEST. The decoded question reads, "Which of north, south, east, or west is 'up' on most maps?"

11. $6 + 1 = 7$

12. The can opener.

It's the only one you usually use two hands to operate.

13. BAFFIN

BORNEO

CYPRUS

HAWAII

HONSHU

SICILY

TAHITI

TAIWAN

14. Expedited, edited

15. 14.

In each grid, the two diagonals add to the same amount.

Test 17

1. PITTANCE
2. DOUBLE TAKE

mile	middle
minus	ominous
sally	usually
clued	clubbed
wordy	worldly
gland	gleaned
wiser	twister
verge	average
icing	kicking
clans	cleanse

3. AS YET and SO FAR
4. DCBA

   The pictures match as homophone pairs:

   rain/rein, Nome/gnome, maze/maize, lynx/links

5. RYES.

   The analogy is in homophones: ALLOWED is to BARRED (antonyms) as SINK is to RISE (also antonyms). We need a homophone of RISE to finish the analogy, so we fill in RYES. (Unfortunately, the word FLOAT does not have a homophone.)

6. LOUD and SOFT

7. The missing word is TOPIC.

Here's the square:

L	A	M	A	S
A	L	O	N	E
T	O	P	I	C
C	H	E	S	T
H	A	D	E	S

8. Raspberry

9. 41.

The top layer has 1 block and needs 15. The second layer has 3 blocks and needs 13. The third layer has 6 blocks and needs 10. The bottom layer has 13 blocks and needs 3. The number of needed blocks is 15 + 13 + 10 + 3 = 41.

10.

Y
30

The letters spell MONOPOLY.

The numbers increase by 1, then 2, then 3, then 4, and so on.

11. ENCRYPTION.

We divided the word into pairs from the front and reversed the order of the letters in each pair.

12. SPEAK.

The replacement letter is A. The words formed are cheAt, Arose, strAw, mediA, chinA. The circled letters spell speck, which can be changed to speAk.

13. 10 photos.

If the 5 people are A, B, C, D, E then the photos needed are ABC, ABD, ABE, ACD, ACE, ADE, BCD, BCE, BDE, CDE.

14. A CAT MAY LOOK AT A KING

15. OVERDO

Test 18

1. M.

The words formed are JAMBS, THEME, and AMBLE.

2. uNEARth & seaFARing

3. 5.

Alternately add and subtract primes: −2 +3 −5 +7 −11 +13 −17 +19 −23 +29 −31.

The calculation: 36 − 31 = 5

4. 80.

The number underneath each clock is the product of the two numbers to which the hands point. Since the last clock has hands pointing at the 10 and the 8, the number underneath it should be 10 × 8 = 80.

5. The cane is the odd one out of these rhymes.

Category: money (honey)

nickel (pickle)

dime (mime)

quarter (mortar)

dollar (collar)

6. REVENGE IS SWEET

7.

8	6	1
4	5	9
2	7	3

The 5 and the 7 must be at the intersection of the only products that are divisible by those two prime numbers. The first column must contain 2, 4, 8 to make a product of 64, and the last column must contain 1, 3, 9 to make a product of 27. The row products indicate the square containing the 8 and 9. Everything falls into place after that.

8. 31 cm.

Remove the decorative base: $208 - 10 = 198$. Subtract 6 shelves (the top of the bookcase and five other planks): $198 - (2 \times 6) = 186$. Divide by 6, since there are 6 spaces for books: $186 \div 6 = 31$.

9. The letter N.

The letter N is the 9th letter in tournameNts, the 3rd letter in coNtests, and the 6th letter in pageaNts.

10.

This answer grid can also be flipped along the main diagonal so that AFGHAN is the first word across.

11. GRAB & TRAP

12. SPARKLING

SPARKING

SPARING

SPRING

SPRIG

PRIG

PIG

PI

I

13. Sunlight

14. CADB

Each word pictured changes its middle letter to form a new word: perch/peach, peony/penny, mouse/moose, house/horse

15. 64 units.

Starting from the bottom left corner and working clockwise, the calculation is 5 + 5 + 11 + 1 + 5 + 5 + 11 + 5 + 5 + 11 = 64.

Test 19

1. 27.

The sequence is 7^7, 6^6, 5^5, 4^4, 3^3, 2^2, 1^1.

The value of 3^3 is 27.

2. RIGGING has the same substitution pattern as VESSELS.

3. BOULEVARD, CHECKMATE, HORSEBACK, MESSENGER

4. B.

A tom repeats to become a tom-tom.

A can repeats to become the cancan.

5. Add U six times to make these countries:

SUDAN, UGANDA, URUGUAY, PERU

6. Y and Z do not appear.

7. DAFFODIL, PANSY, TULIP

8. FRONT ROW SEAT.

FRONT makes "eyes front" and "front door."

ROW makes "skid row" and "row house."

SEAT makes "bicycle seat" and "seat belt."

9. UNI/SEX/TET/HER/BAL/LAD/LES/SON/NET/TLE

10. The car.

It's the only one that isn't round.

11. FAIR & SQUARE

12. 5.

The number in the upper-right square is the product of the numbers in the other three squares.

The calculation: $80 \div 8 \div 2 = 5$

13. FREUD.

Each letter in the first word shifts forward three positions in the alphabet.

14. IGUANA

15. Quizmaster

Test 20

1. CHEDDAR SHREDDER

2. SPONGE

3. 4 sets of three cards.

If 24 is one of the cards, then the other two must add to 51. There are four combinations not including 24 that add to 51: (21,30), (22,29), (23,28), (25,26).

4. E.

Since $1 + 3 + 5 + 7 + 9 = 25$, the wheel turns four full rotations and then one more position. This puts E on the front face.

5. 44.

In the newspaper, lottery numbers are listed in increasing order, and the couple had chosen the six numbers 44, 45, 46, 47, 48, 49 for their ticket. When her husband read 44, she knew that the other five numbers had to match.

6. THOUGH SCHOOLING ENDS, LEARNING DOESN'T.

7. S.

The words formed are ASIDE, PRISM, and HASTE.

8. COMEDY, DRAMA, HORROR, MYSTERY, ROMANCE, SCI-FI, THRILLER

9. RENT & VENT

10. CHIDED.

Each card represents two letters. The first letter is the position of the card's value in the alphabet, and the second is C, D, H, or S for its suit. The last word deciphers as:

3 of hearts = C + H

9 of diamonds = I + D

5 of diamonds = E + D

11. 609.

To get the next term, add the previous two terms and add one.

The calculation: 232 + 376 + 1 = 609

12. CREAM

13. Hip, jaw, rib

(Other answers are possible.)

14. TESTIMONY, SOFA, HEATHENS.

The play is *Timon of Athens*.

15. Sweets.

Each word in the sentence is inside a shape with the same number of sides. The only word among the choices with six letters is "sweets."

INDEX

_____

The numbers indicate the test number and the question number. The letters in front indicate which section the test is from. Verbal Tests have a VB, Visual Tests a VS, Numerical Tests a N, and Calculation and Logic Tests have a CL. No letter indicates that the test comes from the last section, the IQ Testers.